THE COUGAR LADY

THE COUGAR LADY

Legendary Trapper of Sechelt Inlet

ROSELLA LESLIE

CAITLIN PRESS

02 03 04 05 06 24 23 22 21 20

Caitlin Press Inc.
8100 Alderwood Road,
Halfmoon Bay, BC V0N 1Y1
caitlin-press.com

Text design by Kathleen Fraser.
Cover design by Vici Johnstone.
Edited by Betty Keller.

Printed in Canada on FSC-certified paper using 100 percent post-consumer waste. The paper is acid- and chlorine-free and is ancient-forest friendly.

Caitlin Press Inc. acknowledges financial support from the Government of Canada through the Canada Book Fund and the Canada Council for the Arts, and from the Province of British Columbia through the British Columbia Arts Council and the Book Publisher's Tax Credit.

Funded by the Government of Canada | Canada

Library and Archives Canada Cataloguing in Publication

Leslie, Rosella M., 1948–, author
The cougar lady : legendary trapper of Sechelt Inlet / Rosella Leslie.

ISBN 978-1-927575-63-5 (pbk.)

1. Solberg, Bergie. 2. Trappers—British Columbia—Sechelt—Biography. 3. Trapping—British Columbia—Sechelt. 4. Outdoor life—British Columbia—Sechelt. 5. Sechelt (B.C.)—Biography. I. Title.

SK283.6.C2L47 2014 639'.1092 C2014-904122-5

This book is dedicated to the memory
of Bergliot and Minnie Solberg
and the Sunshine Coast community
that they enriched.

CONTENTS

Bergie's goat herd at Carlson Creek provided her with all the milk she needed but also attracted predators. To protect them she fought cougars and bears and was not above stealing them back from new owners who didn't treat them right. Photo courtesy of Bill Walkey.

INTRODUCTION

Asta Bergliot Solberg was always called Bergliot by her parents and sister, but she was known as "Bergie" to her friends, and for a while, by those who didn't know better, as "Myrtle." Her Cougar Lady nickname came from Jim Wilkinson, an amateur ham radio operator who retired to the Sunshine Coast in 1981. At that time Bergie was living at Carlson Creek on the west side of Sechelt Inlet.

"I went fishing one morning," Jim related, "and passing by her place saw that the door to her cabin was open. There was no smoke and the dog was barking."

When he returned after two hours of fishing, nothing had changed, so he went ashore. The place was cold, there was no food and Bergie was lying ill in a back bedroom.

"It seemed ridiculous to me that this aging woman was so isolated and had no way of communicating with the outside world," said Jim.

Back at his own home he dug out an old citizen's band (CB) radio, antennas and a car battery and a few days later,

Bergie hunted alone in the mountains above Jervis, Salmon, Sechelt and Narrows inlets, often spending nights in the wilderness with only her gun and one of her Norwegian elkhounds for protection. Carlson Creek, photo courtesy of Bill Walkey.

with the help of his son-in-law, Steve Day, hooked the system up in Bergie's cabin. To use the CB, Bergie needed a handle. Jim's was "Tranquility," and he suggested that hers might be "Bear Lady."

"She didn't like that," he explained, "because it might be mistaken for 'bare lady,' so I said what about 'Cougar Lady'? Well, she liked that one and that is how she came to be called the Cougar Lady of the Inlet."

It was an apt name for a woman who had spent most of her life in the woods, who had climbed treacherous mountain trails in pursuit of wild goats, and who had wrestled with bears and cougars.

While she augmented her living by hunting, trapping and fishing, Bergie's main income came from the logging industry. She started as a whistlepunk for the Osborne Logging Company Ltd., a job that entailed sending signals from the cut area to the yarder via a switchbox attached to a long electric cable. In order to stay close enough to the chokerman to hear his commands, she had to scramble over limbs and stumps; avoid hidden holes; be wary of powerful steel cables whipping over the slash, threatening to trip, cut or decapitate anything in their path; and watch out for airborne logs that could swing and twist in any direction, their limbs and tops frequently breaking off, sometimes flying into the air, then slamming back down to the ground. On rainy days, squeezing the switchbox often caused twelve volts of electricity to shoot through her hand.

Whenever the rigging crew moved to a new cut, Bergie would help gather cables, including the straw line, which was used to haul heavier cables and which ranged from one inch to one-and-a-quarter inches in diameter.

If Bergie's boat's motor was broken or she had no gas, she would row a boat to wherever she needed to go, sometimes even from Deserted Bay to Egmont, a trip well over sixty kilometres. At Carlson Creek, her junk collection included old boats, defunct washing machines, two Volkswagen Beetles and a Triumph motorcycle. Photo courtesy of Randy Thomas and the *Vancouver Sun.*

"It was about the only time she'd wear gloves," said Robert Lemieux, who worked with Bergie at one of Gus Crucil's logging camps. "But even then she sometimes wouldn't and her hands would get all cut up."

One of his most vivid memories of Bergie originated during one of these rigging moves.

"It was important to keep the cables clear of everything so they didn't get damaged," he said. "That afternoon Bergie came in with about a thousand feet of wire around her neck. She was sopping wet and her hair was tangled up in the wire. It was all I could do to lift that wire off myself. That cable was always spliced, and normally the person hauling would take the splices apart. I asked her why she didn't undo the splices and bring it in smaller rolls, and she said she didn't want to make that many trips. But I think it was because she could never find the tool she needed to take the splices apart."

Often Bergie combined her work as a whistlepunk with a camp-watching job.

Betty Laidlaw told of a time when her husband, Ed, and brother-in-law, Art Asseltine, heard that Bergie was keeping a bear cub as a pet at a camp she was looking after.

"Art and Ed went to Sechelt Creek one day to see Bergie. She said she had a bear cub. She'd fought it down the hill and into a shed."

Bergie asked if the two men would like to see the cub, and when they agreed, she led the way into the shed. There was no light and she couldn't see the bear.

"Oh, gosh," she said. "Where did it go?"

Then they heard a growl up in the rafters.

"There was her 'baby,'" said Ed. "It was a two-year-old bear! Bergie was all covered in scratches."

Bergie's fiery temper resulted in some dramatic encounters with local law enforcement officers. In 1979, shortly after his arrival on the coast, conservation officer James A. Stephen Jr. (known as Jamie) caught her with two fresh bearskins but no licence. As part of his investigation, it was necessary for him to confiscate her weapons. Bergie was fifty-six and living in a trailer as night watchperson for Jackson Brothers Logging at Gray Creek. It was close to suppertime when Stephen arrived with a warrant to search the premises, but having heard stories about Bergie "decking loggers," he had asked for an RCMP backup. Unfortunately, just as they arrived, the officer received a radio call to deal with a domestic dispute and the conservation officer was left alone. When it became clear that one of the rifles he was about to confiscate was the Winchester she had inherited from her father, Bergie flew into a rage.

"In the confines of that small trailer," said Stephen, "it was a very, very unpleasant scene. She'd been cooking and had a pot of scalding soup or dog food on the stove, and she actually threw that at me. It degenerated from there and we both ended up outside, and we had a tug-of-war for the gun. I ultimately subdued her and seized the .30-30."

However, it was the hair-raising stories of Bergie's cougar encounters that endorsed her nickname. One of these, as told by Sunshine Coast logger Mike Jackson, resulted from a trip Bergie and her parents took to Norway. "They had a fellow look after their place. I guess he was going through their stuff and he got to fooling around with the guns, including Bergie's favourite gun. Some time after the family returned Bergie was out in the woods and came across a cougar kill. A few moments later she came upon the cougar. She slipped a shell into the gun and went to shoot, but the gun jammed."

Bergie never forgave the man, and she'd repeat the story to anyone who would listen.

"I went to kill a cougar and my gun wouldn't work!" she told Jackson. "The cougar jumped at me and I had to hit it with the stock of my gun!"

According to Jackson, the man steered clear of Bergie from that day on.

In many ways Bergliot Solberg was as wary, agile and uncivilized as a cougar, and like the big cats, her public reviews were mixed. She was despised by folks she had exploited, slandered or cheated; she was avoided by those who were repulsed by her eccentric habits, coarse appearance and earthy smell; and she was used by those who found her an amusing diversion, a story to be told over a beer or a travel anecdote to be shared back home. However, those who counted themselves as friends saw beyond Bergie's rough exterior. They had witnessed her vulnerability, compassion, courage and determination, and their lives had been enriched by the Cougar Lady of Sechelt Inlet.

BEGINNINGS

Bergliot Solberg's life was greatly influenced by the history of her birth country and the immigration policies of both Canada and the United States. Her father, Herman Nikolai Solberg, was born on November 29, 1891, and grew up in the seaport city of Drammen in southern Norway, which was a major railroad junction and home to pulp, cellulose and paper industries, as well as mining, shipbuilding and salmon fishing. Her mother, Olga Solberg (née Moen), was born on May 4, 1896, in Sandsvær, which is now a part of Kongsberg, a small city on the Lågen River.

By the time he had reached manhood, Herman Solberg proved to be the type of person who would tackle almost any job that came his way. Although many of his countrymen were unemployed, as a railroad worker he had no trouble finding employment. With the completion of the huge Oslo–Bergen line in 1909, however, even railroad jobs became scarce.

Tempted by letters from relatives in Minnesota where the economy was booming, especially in the farming sector, Herman

NEW LANDS BECKONING

In 1801 roughly 80 percent of Norway's citizens were engaged in farming even though less than 3 percent of the country was arable. With so little land available, it became the custom for the eldest son to inherit the family's holdings, leaving his siblings to seek jobs as labourers with almost no hope of ever owning their own farms. By 1850, although the country was in the throes of an agricultural and industrial revolution, the population had almost doubled and there were still more workers than jobs. As a consequence, during the last half of the century more than five hundred thousand Norwegians emigrated to North America, enticed by offers of free land.

In 1896, to compete with the United States in attracting immigrants to the sparsely settled prairies, the Canadian Ministry of the Interior launched a massive advertising campaign that was actively supported by shipping and railway companies and their agents, who were paid a commission for every settler they brought to the country. The resulting propaganda included misleading posters of bountiful wheat fields, enormous fruit and vegetable displays and modern homesteads. Territories competing for these immigrants added to the deceptions, sometimes with maps that placed the Maritime provinces next to the North Pole and the

Canadian prairies close to the subtropics. Deceitful as it was, the strategy worked, and according to T.K. Derry in *A History of Modern Norway 1814–1977*, "by 1921 Canadians of Norwegian stock numbered nearly 70,000, of whom four-fifths lived on, and presumably by, the land."[1]

began making plans to emigrate to America. Before these plans could materialize, however, the world became embroiled in war; leaving his homeland was now out of the question.

Largely as a result of Norway's shipping industry, the war resulted in an economic boom and an increase in the job market, but unfortunately for Herman, the boom did not last.

For a brief while immediately following the war, the economy in Norway once again improved, but in the fall of 1920 the country went into a recession that lasted for the next two decades. Unemployment rose to 8 percent and even those with a higher education than Herman had trouble finding work. As US immigrant Arnfinn Bruflot is quoted as saying by the author of *New Land, New Lives*:

> After the first World War was very good times. So everybody thought, well, get yourself an education and then you've got it made. But it didn't turn out that way. By the middle '20s there already had gotten to be a surplus of teachers and almost any occupation you could think of. I had borrowed a lot of money [for education] and I had to do something to pay back the bank. So the only way I could take care of my responsibilities and meet my obligations, why I had to emigrate.[2]

NORWAY IN WORLD WAR I

At the outbreak of World War I, Norway's merchant marine fleet was the fourth-largest in the world. Although the country remained neutral, in exchange for Britain's protection of the fleet, the Norwegian government granted privileges to Britain and its allies. While some ships were still lost to mine fields and German patrols that confiscated and destroyed vessels whenever they suspected the cargo was bound for Allied ports, the enormous profits made by the shipping industry caused a surge in Norway's economy. This ended in 1917 when Germany declared war on non-friendly vessels, and the United States, suspicious of the Scandinavian neutrality, imposed a trade embargo on Denmark, Sweden and Norway, resulting in an economic downturn, food shortages and rationing in those countries.

The embargo did not stop the US from using Norwegian ships such as the SS *Imo*, which stopped for refuelling in Halifax on December 6, 1917. The *Imo* was on its way to New York to pick up relief supplies for Belgium and as it was leaving the Halifax harbour it was rammed by the SS *Mont Blanc*, a French cargo ship loaded with munitions. The resulting explosion—with a force equivalent to the release of three kilotons of TNT—combined with fires set by flaming debris raining down upon the city, and a tsunami triggered by the shock waves, killed more than fifteen hundred people, injured nine thousand others and destroyed or damaged every building within twenty-five kilometres.

By the war's end, 1,892 Norwegian merchant sailors had died and 50 percent of the country's merchant fleet had been destroyed.

Herman had made the same choice, but his plans were once again thwarted, this time by a temporary quota act[3] that had been passed by the United States Congress limiting the number of people who would be allowed into the country. As a result, instead of Minnesota, Herman turned his sights on Canada.

While the Canadian government was arguing over its immigration policy, the North Atlantic steamship combine was creating another hurdle in the path of would-be immigrants by raising freight and passenger rates to Canadian ports by as much as 700 percent. A family consisting of two parents and five children who could have secured passage from England or the continent for $122.50 in 1900 were now being charged $600 for the same journey.[4]

This amounted to a small fortune for Herman Solberg, who was now married to Olga Moen and the father of two children: Minnie, born on August 16, 1922, and Asta Bergliot, born on September 5, 1923. With four people to support and jobs in Norway becoming harder and harder to obtain, his

2

(Reglm. § 36, 61.)

Ved utskrivningsmøtet for ....

den 25/6 1918 kjendt: ....

Krigskommissær.

Utskrevet til ....

bataljon (korps, befæstning, sjøvæbningen) med

matr.nr. ——— 19

3

Lægebedømmelse.

(Her anføres for hver gang bedømmelse foretages: sted, tid, resultat, oplysninger, som antages at være av betydning for senere bedømmelse samt ansvarshavende læges navn. For alle sjøfarende anføres om farveblind eller ikke.) Reglm. §§ 33, 61, 98.

Første undersøkelse:

Høide 177 cm.; andet, som antages at ha betydning:

Obs.! «K», «Fla», «Ing.», «Fsa» o. s. v. betyder blot: dygtig til kavaleriet, feltartillriet o. s. v. Resultatet av utskrivningen kan bli et andet!

Senere undersøkelser:

Although Norway remained neutral during World War I, it was compulsory for all men between the ages of eighteen and twenty-six to serve in the national militia. Herman's military papers may also have served as his passport. Author photo.

dream of emigrating to Canada seemed to be slipping farther from his grasp.

Unknowingly, Herman was helped in his quest when British shipping magnate Sir William Petersen offered to use his fleet of ten vessels to take care of Canada's shipping needs at reasonable rates, forcing the North Atlantic combine to negotiate with the Liberal government and lower their rates.

As Canada's economy began to improve, the Liberals simplified the immigration process and almost doubled the number of immigrants allowed into the country. Preference was given to farm workers and domestic servants and to people from the "preferred countries of northern Europe and Scandinavia."[5]

THE DESIRABLE IMMIGRANT

After World War I the Canadian economy was in turmoil as a result of returned soldiers looking for jobs, unions demanding higher wages and manufacturers fighting for tariff protection to restrict imports of low-cost foreign goods. The Conservative opposition cried for a slowdown in immigration until increased tariffs could rebuild the economy. The Liberal government, led by the Right Honourable W.L. Mackenzie King and which had been elected to power at the end of 1920, insisted that opening up western farmlands through increased immigration would ease Canada's economic woes. But even the Liberals were selective in their choice of "desirable" immigrants.

Sir Henry Worth Thornton, president and chairman of the Canadian National Railway, told the New York Board of Trade and Transportation in 1925 that, while settlers were welcome to Canada, they must be healthy and capable of supporting themselves and their families so as not to become a burden on taxpayers, be Caucasian because "Canada wants no race problems," and be prepared to abide by Canada's laws and social expectations. Thornton was adamant that Canada wanted "no such disturbers of society as Bolsheviks and Communists."[6]

What Canada wanted most was immigrants from the United States and Great Britain who were considered "superior types." Northern and western Europeans were the second choice, followed by eastern Europeans and finally southern Europeans.

This was the opportunity Herman had been waiting for, and his application for immigration as a Norwegian farmer was approved by the Canadian immigration authorities.

On August 31, 1926, Herman, Olga, Minnie and Bergliot travelled to Oslo where they boarded the Wilson Line's 861-passenger *Calypso*, a two-masted, 3,817-ton steamship, which took them to Liverpool, England. Three days later, on September 3, they boarded the Canadian Pacific steamship *Montrose*, bound for Canada.

Built in 1922, the SS *Montrose* held 1,810 passengers and travelled at a top speed of 16 knots. The Solbergs were travelling in the third-class section. Their four-berth stateroom was small but comfortable and contained two dressers, a washstand and mirrors. Lavatories were located along a passageway and shared with other passengers.

The weather was fair the day they left England, with only a slight swell as they crossed the Irish Sea to Belfast and then journeyed up the Firth of Clyde to Greenock before heading out to the open Atlantic. There were only six other Norwegians on board the *Montrose*, the majority of the third-class passengers being Ukrainian immigrants from Poland. There were also a great number of English boys from ages fourteen to nineteen who were immigrating under

On September 3, 1926, the Solberg family boarded the CPR's SS *Montrose* in Liverpool and set off for their new lives in Canada. Photo courtesy of heritage-ships.com.

the auspices of the Salvation Army. Thus the dining room, although huge, was a noisy place to be at mealtimes, but since the tables were limited to six people, the Solbergs only had to share theirs with two others.

During the eight-day journey across the Atlantic, third-class passengers spent much of the time on the deck, watching or playing shuffleboard or deck quoits, or sitting in the large public rooms. There were also dances and concerts held each evening.

On September 11, Herman and his family joined their fellow immigrants on deck as the *Montrose* moved slowly up the St. Lawrence to the Port of Quebec. The day was fair, the temperature reaching a high of 18°C. When docking was completed, the passengers were herded into the great hallway of the customs building. It was crowded with immigrants and officials, talking and shouting in different languages. Although on the *Montrose* passenger manifests Olga was listed as being able to read English, like many of her fellow immigrants, her comprehension of the language was limited. It would have been difficult for her to read the direction signs posted in the hallway and at the same time keep track of her two small daughters, Minnie, now four, and Bergie, three.

In the end, it was probably the crowd that pushed them toward the appropriate customs lineup where they waited until it was their turn to present their papers and the medical certificates they'd received in Norway to the customs officer. He would have stamped their passports and directed them to a Scandinavian interpreter who was on hand to assist newly arrived immigrants.

On his immigration application, Herman had listed himself as a farmer, but he had no intention of settling on the prairies. Many of the immigrants who had given up and returned to Norway had brought with them stories of living in sod houses until they could afford to buy the lumber they needed to build a proper home, of cold winters with little fuel for heating, spring thaws that left roads impassable, and summer droughts. Instead, he chose to settle on the west coast which was said to be much like Norway, with its deep fjords, thick forests and endless opportunities for hunting and fishing. Fortunately, he arrived with $150 cash—enough money to pay for their transport to British Columbia. After making their way through the customs building, he and his family boarded a train bound for Montreal, where they connected with a CPR colonist train to Vancouver.

Used to transport immigrants across Canada, colonist cars were first built in 1884 and used until the 1950s. Each car consisted of sixteen to twenty open sections which could be transformed into lower and upper berths with no mattresses, the colonists being expected to bring their own bedding. There were no curtains or partitions to separate them from their fellow travellers, and while the children fell asleep easily, the noise of the train and the anxious mutterings from fellow passengers in a multitude of languages must have discouraged sleep for the adults. They were entering a world completely alien to that which they'd known in Europe, and most were facing it with a mixture of anticipation, apprehension and sorrow for the loved ones they had left behind.

Olga would not have been able to express any doubts she may have had about the venture to Herman. Tall and gruff, he was an autocratic man who believed that, as head of the family, he was to be honoured, obeyed and never questioned. She had been raised in the traditional Norwegian fashion to believe that a woman's role was to follow her husband, look after his needs and accept his leadership. The fact that she was also raised as a lady and had received an education meant nothing. Still, it would have been surprising on that long train ride toward an uncertain future if she hadn't longed for her homeland, where everything was familiar and she had parents and siblings to support her.

For five days the train rumbled westward, stopping frequently at towns and villages where immigrant families would disembark, their stoic expressions hiding their fear and bewilderment. The train crossed the mountains at night and when the Solbergs woke on the morning of the fifth day, they were travelling through the forests and farmlands of the Fraser Valley.

While Olga, Bergie and Minnie were happy living in a North Pacific Lumber Company house where they enjoyed modern conveniences and the companionship of other Norwegian families, Herman longed for the wilderness. Photo by Philip Timms, courtesy of Vancouver Public Library 7059.

The train station in Vancouver was located very close to the city's Norwegian community and it was here that Herman and his family spent their first night. In the morning, following the advice of his countrymen, he rode the "Toonerville Trolley" to the end of the line at Hastings and Ellesmere, then walked along the gravelled Hastings Street to reach the North Pacific mill at Barnet, where he secured a job on the green chain and a company house for himself and his family.

Built in 1889 by James MacLaren and James Ross, the huge North Pacific Lumber Company mill sprawled next to the shore on the south side of Burrard Inlet. In 1926 it was one of the largest sawmills in the British Empire and was

BARNET AND THE "TOONERVILLE TROLLEY"

Just 14.5 kilometres east of Vancouver, Barnet was part of the Municipality of Burnaby, which is sandwiched between the cities of Vancouver and New Westminster. This heavily forested area had been opened for settlement in 1891 when Canada's first electric tramline, the interurban, was constructed by the BC Electric Company to transport freight and passengers between the two cities.

A Vancouver streetcar known as the "dinky" ran along Hastings Street on a single track, and when in 1913 the tramline was extended into north Burnaby, the "dinky" was nicknamed the "Toonerville Trolley," after a popular comic strip.

certainly much bigger than the mills in which Herman had occasionally worked in Norway.

The green chain—a conveyor system onto which the milled lumber drops after it leaves the trim saw—is situated at the end of a log's journey through a sawmill. Workers pull the lumber off the chain, then sort and stack it by length and thickness. Because the wood is green, it is always heavy and it takes a man with a strong back to handle it. At first Herman was just such a man.

Minnie and Bergie were happy to have a home once more, a place that didn't bump and jostle them, where they could

CHARLES EDWARD BURT

Charles Edward Burt was born in Kongsburg, Norway, in 1873 and christened Gustav Elvesaeter, but for unknown reasons he changed his name. At the age of eight he emigrated to the United States where he worked for a time in a Wisconsin logging camp. As Charles Burt, he joined the 2nd Wisconsin Volunteer Infantry and fought with Teddy Roosevelt's Rough Riders in the Spanish-American War. When that conflict was over, he tried ranching in Idaho, then went to Mexico to fight with the revolutionary Pancho Villa, a move that made him unwelcome in the United States.

Burt was heading for Kamloops to start a cattle ranch when World War I was declared and he immediately changed plans and joined the Canadian Army. Wounded and gassed at Ypres, he was demobilized in England, where he met and married Lizzie Coysh. When the war was over, they went to Edmonton, but according to his son, the late William H. Burt, it was so cold that he didn't even bother to get off the train. Instead he went on to Barnet, BC, where he obtained a job at the Nichols Chemical Company sulphuric acid plant.

go inside or out at will, and most of all, a place where they would stay put. Throughout the following spring and summer, they joined the children of other mill workers and spent hours playing along the shores of Burrard Inlet.

Most of the Solbergs' neighbours were also immigrants, many of them from Norway. One of these was Charles Burt, a watchman at the nearby Nichols Chemical Company sulphuric acid plant. According to his son, the late William "Grizz" Burt, Charles was the kind of man who liked to help people out and although he was much older than Herman, they soon became good friends.

For two years the Solbergs lived in Burnaby, and their lives seemed secure. The work at the mill was steady, and Herman quickly picked up the English he needed to communicate with his employers and fellow workers. Restricted by her own limitations with the new language, Olga preferred to socialize with other Norwegian ladies in the neighbourhood, but Bergie and Minnie began to learn English from other children.

During this time Herman heard Charles Burt talk about his visits to a pre-emption (a lot the Crown offered Burt at a low price before it became available for general sale, a provision of the Dominion Lands Act) at Four Mile Point on Sechelt Inlet. Homesteaded by Burt's stepdaughter and her husband, it was the kind of place Herman dreamed of owning, a place where a man could be his own boss and earn his living off the land by hunting, fishing and trapping.

Olga, however, was happy in the city. It was a world she knew, a world in which she could safely raise her daughters, where they could be educated and grow up to find good husbands. But this idyllic existence was shattered when one day in the spring of 1928 Herman damaged his back pulling a heavy plank from the green chain. He was unable to work, and by the time he recovered from his injury, his job had been taken by someone else.

The Solbergs joined the throng of travellers gathered at the Union Steamship docks at the foot of Carrall Street in Vancouver to board the steamship to Sechelt. Photo by Leonard Frank, courtesy of Vancouver Public Library 2763.

Since he no was longer employed by the mill, Herman lost the right to live in the house on East Hastings Street. The family moved to a smaller house on North Road near what is now the Barnet Highway, a place much farther from the shops and neighbours. Here Herman faced a problem much greater than losing his job.

As a result of Canada's Naturalization Act of 1914, it was necessary for immigrants to reside in the country for five years before they could apply for naturalization. At any time prior to naturalization they could be deported if they became

In 1928 the Solberg family boarded the Union Steamship's *Lady Cynthia* and steamed toward their new home on the shores of Sechelt Inlet. Photographer unknown, courtesy of Vancouver Public Library 31879.

"physically or mentally disabled, sick or diseased, alcoholics, criminals, paupers ... or relied on public charity for support."[7] In 1925 approximately 40 percent of deportations from Canada were immigrants who could no longer support themselves. If Herman did not find work soon, he and his family would be deported.

It was Charles Burt who came to his rescue.

"My stepdaughter wants to move off the homestead," he told Herman. "You could take it over. All you have to do is make $250 worth of improvements over five years and the property is yours."

For Herman, this was a dream come true and he readily agreed to the plan.

With the help of Burt and his sons, the Solbergs' belongings, including a beautiful chest that had been part of Olga's dowry, were loaded onto a wagon and transported with the family to the *Lady Cynthia* berthed at the Union Steamship's Carrall Street wharf in Vancouver. When their possessions were stowed in the cargo section below decks, the family boarded the upper decks. The gangplanks were lifted and the steamship slowly left the harbour, headed toward a part of the country where Herman would feel completely at home, where Olga would be forever alienated and where Minnie and Bergliot would spend the rest of their lives.

ADAPTING TO A ROUGH WORLD

As the *Lady Cynthia* approached the pier jutting out into Trail Bay off the tiny village of Sechelt, the Solbergs would have seen to their right a hotel and a cluster of houses dominated by the ornate white tower of the Sechelt Indian Band's Our Lady of Lourdes church, built in 1907. Along the waterfront to the left of the pier were the Union Steamship general store, post office, telephone exchange, dance pavilion, teahouse and summer cottages.

The majority of Sechelt village residents worked for the Union Steamship Company or in the fishing and logging industries. Since there were no roads joining the Sunshine Coast to the rest of the mainland, there were few automobiles, and the local roads that did exist in 1928 were roughly built and riddled with potholes. As a result, most travel on this part of the coast was accomplished by boat, either via Sechelt Inlet or along Georgia Strait.

As the Solbergs walked down the Trail Bay wharf, they could see to their left the dance pavilion and general store and to their right the second Sechelt Hotel. Photo c. 1926–1928 by Edric Clayton, courtesy of Sechelt Community Archives.

It was normal for a cluster of passengers and townspeople to gather on the wharf when the steamship docked, and since the arrival of permanent residents was infrequent, a new family would have attracted interest. The Solbergs would have stood out in the crowd—Herman almost six feet tall, blond, blue-eyed and muscular, albeit slightly stooped; Olga, also blue-eyed, but with light brown hair pulled neatly back from her plump face and fastened in a tight roll; and two little girls, both as blond and blue-eyed as their father.

The Solbergs had never been to Sechelt before, but William Burt believed that his father had provided a map and directions to the homestead, and he made arrangements for Herman to rent a boat. Even so, Herman would have faced a monumental task in transporting the family's belongings along the dirt road from the Trail Bay wharf across the eight-hundred-metre isthmus that separates Trail Bay on Georgia Strait from Porpoise Bay on Sechelt Inlet to a second dock. From there, they travelled by boat to their new home on Sechelt Inlet, 6.4 kilometres north of the village.

The Solbergs' 72.8-acre homestead (District Lot 4679) was situated on the east side of the inlet and covered the whole of Four Mile Point. It was characterized by steep hills, dense forest and a small piece of flat land on the north side of the point where two cabins that had been built by the Burt family were located.

"There was a well and two one-room shiplap cabins near the shore," remembered William Burt, who, as a boy, spent two summers with the Solbergs. "There wasn't very much to them so Herman went to work and built a lean-to for the kitchen in the one they lived in."

Eventually, Herman also built himself a fourteen-foot rowboat.

"He used fir and it was a heavy son-of-a-gun," said Burt. "You could stand on the gunnels and it would never tip over."

For young Bergie and Minnie, Four Mile Point was a paradise. They were outside from morning till night, exploring the woods and playing on the beach. Susan Cocks remembered that her mother, the late Dorothy Clode (née Chamberlain), was fascinated by the way Bergie and Minnie could both run across barnacles in bare feet.

THE INLAND SEA

Sechelt Inlet, a twenty-three-kilometre land-locked waterway known as the Inland Sea, is one of the major inlets of the British Columbia coast. Fed by waters from both Georgia Strait and Jervis Inlet that flow through the Skookumchuck Narrows, it angles in a southeasterly direction toward Sechelt village. Along the way, two additional waterways branch farther inland—Narrows Inlet, which branches fifteen kilometres in a northeasterly direction to the Tzoonie River, and Salmon Inlet, which branches twenty-three kilometres eastward to Clowhom Falls.

Boaters entering the Skookumchuck Narrows on an active tide face one of the world's most treacherous saltwater rapids where current speeds can reach more than thirty kilometres per hour and whirlpools can turn and capsize even a sturdy vessel in a matter of minutes. During a slack tide, however, which lasts about twenty minutes, this same waterway grows so calm that boaters can row safely from one end to the other. Many lives have been lost as a result of inexperience or misjudging the tides. In the late 1930s three young girls from Doriston started through the Skookumchuck in a rowboat on their way to purchase a bucket of ice cream from the Takai & Maeda Store in Egmont. They never reached the store and neither they nor their boat were ever seen again.

But rapids are not the only danger posed by the Inland Sea, where calm waters can turn into a frenzy of wild winds and white-capped waves. On April 13, 1960, six loggers were drowned in just such a gale. The storm was already brewing when the crew left the Morrison Logging Camp on the west side of Sechelt Inlet for the Porpoise Bay dock, eight miles to the south. Their boat was found empty the next morning, swamped by waves resulting from sixty-mile-per-hour wind gusts.

William Burt was equally amazed.

"In April they'd take their shoes off and they wouldn't put them back on again until October," he marvelled. "They used to chase up and down the beach that way!"

Shortly after moving to Four Mile Point—later renamed Sandy Hook by the developer Capilano Highlands Ltd.—Herman was hired by Robert and Anne Chamberlain to cut wood and make minor repairs to their summer house. Bergie and Minnie would often accompany him when he went to work, and Bergie soon formed a friendship with Dorothy Chamberlain that would last the rest of their lives.

"My mom envied these girls who didn't have to go to school," said Dorothy's eldest daughter, Elizabeth Clode. "Herman didn't believe in educating girls."

Sechelt school trustees had already tried to convince Herman that the girls should be enrolled in the local school located at what is now the corner of Winter Avenue and Norwest Bay Road in West Sechelt. But even when several

CARLSON CREEK

Carlson Creek originates at Carlson Lake and flows eastward until it empties into the west side of Sechelt Inlet just south of Piper Point.

On August 28, 1909, Swedish-born Herman Carlson pre-empted Lot 3047 between "Little Rocky Point" (Piper Point) and the outcrop known today as Carlson Point. Although he died two years later, his wife, Otilia, with the help of their five sons, was able to make the improvements that enabled her to receive a crown grant for the property in 1913. By that time the homestead included the family house, workshops, storerooms, stables, hay barns, chicken houses and fourteen acres under cultivation.

Soon after the outbreak of World War I, the Carlson family moved to the United States, and a few years later the buildings and property were purchased as a summer home by Robert and Anne Chamberlain. Robert was an electrical engineer who had been responsible for wiring the Hotel Vancouver, the Marine Building and the Stanley Theatre. The family owned a large house on Burrard Street in what is now downtown Vancouver, where Anne raised chickens, goats and bees.

Every summer, Anne would hire a barge, load it with her household goods, chickens, goats and bees, and have it towed up the Strait of Georgia, through Agamemnon Channel and the Skookumchuck Narrows to Carlson Creek. With Anne came her daughter, Dorothy, who was born in 1919, and her son, Fred, as well as several orphaned children.

Sechelt residents offered free board for the girls during the week, Herman refused, although he did finally agree to send for correspondence courses. When William Burt stayed with the family during the summer of 1930, he often assisted the girls with their lessons.

"I don't know how Minnie did, but Bergie was very handicapped in writing or anything like that. They were outdoors all the time."

Although many local residents believed that Olga had been a teacher, in a 1991 interview Bergie insisted that this wasn't so.

"That's what everybody says, but she never was. 'Course, she teached me and Minnie, but she never was a schoolteacher. And then my father would teach us. We had correspondence at home, so we learned to read and write that way. You see, the school was too far out. It was way up in West Sechelt, not right in Sechelt like it is now. Then we never had a motor boat. We had to row. So my father said it's too far for us to row every morning and every night."

But Olga's tutelage did influence her daughters, for the Norwegian that Bergie and Minnie spoke was both fluent and educated.

"When I listened to the two of them speaking Norwegian back and forth, it was picture perfect," said Tor Skei, who came from Norway to the coast as a boy in 1967. "Then all of a sudden, they slipped into a dialect."

"Sometimes if I have to talk to Norwegians and stuff like that I can change right over from English if I want to," said Bergie.

Joan O'Shea (née Chambers), who knew the Solbergs in later years, remembered how keen Bergie and Minnie were to learn. "My first memory of speaking to Bergie was when I was sitting on the front step. She came into the yard and started talking. She was really proud to have learned how to tell time. And she said she could read. She took off her hat and read the writing on it."

William Burt and other people who knew Herman maintained that he was always bitter because he had no sons. As a consequence, they said, he demanded that Minnie and Bergie fulfill that role, helping him clear the land and participating in his efforts to feed and clothe his family.

Although the Solbergs' Four Mile Point property had been logged of its prime timber in earlier years, there were still enough cedar, hemlock and second-growth fir trees remaining for Herman to earn some income handlogging. After felling the trees with an axe and a crosscut saw, he created a "skid" of smaller trees—arranged vertically going down the hill—like a railroad track without ties. A smooth surface was created by scraping the bark from the skids and greasing them with dogfish oil, and a Gilchrist jack and a peavey were used to lift a log onto the skids. If all went well, the log would roll down the skid and into the water. Later the girls would row the boat while Herman rounded up the logs, pounded "dogs"—large-eyed spikes—into the butts, and roped them together to form a boom.

Robert and Anne Chamberlain at their home on Chilco Street in Vancouver, 1943. Bergie was a frequent visitor at their Carlson Creek summer home and formed a lifelong friendship with their daughter, Dorothy Chamberlain Clode. Photo courtesy of Elizabeth Clode.

Anne and Robert Chamberlain spent their summers at their Carlson Creek farm, hiring Herman to do odd jobs. Photo courtesy of Elizabeth Clode.

"They helped their father skid the logs into the water," wrote reporter Nancy Moote in a 1995 article in *Coastlife*, "and [Bergie] vividly remembers how red snappers would float up, stunned by the force of the splashing logs."[8]

The girls were also recruited to help Herman clear land for a garden, pulling out alder saplings, salal and salmonberry bushes. Larger stumps were either burned or removed with stumping powder. Once it was cleared of trees and brush, the family faced the arduous task of removing large rocks and hauling seaweed from the beach to enrich the gravelly soil.

Drawing on their farming experience in Norway, securing advice and cuttings from the Chamberlains and their neighbours, Jiro (Jim) and Hanna Konishi, and scrounging other cuttings or plants from homesteads that had been abandoned up and down the inlet, Herman and Olga soon had a huge garden and orchard. In the summer of 1930, William Burt helped Herman dig out a plum tree from an abandoned homestead near McLean Bay.

"Solberg dug it out and we towed it up to Four Mile behind the boat," said Burt. "Then he went out and got a net full of dogfish and dug a big hole and planted the tree and put the dogfish in."

When Burt returned as an adult with his own children, the plum tree was so weighed down with fruit that every branch had to be supported.

Whenever he could not sell his logs or there was no other work available, Herman turned to handlining to make a few cents.

"He used to fish the dogfish and take the liver," Bergie said. "Then he fished sockeye salmon."

Like most of the handliners of his day, Herman scrounged

his tackle from whatever was at hand—leads mooched from local gillnetters and a coil of green cotton line.

"We used piano wire as leaders," said William Burt, "and we'd get brass and copper and make our own spoons on a block of wood."

Because the length of his line was limited, Herman usually fished the shallow kelp beds where salmon liked to hide, but sometimes he fished off the rock bluffs where cod and dogfish were plentiful. When the herring were running, he, Minnie and Bergie would go out with a dip net and a bucket and collect enough for dinner and for bait. When herring weren't available, they baited their hooks with bits of mussel or clam.

Securing the free end of the line to his thigh, Herman would lower his baited hook into the water until it touched the bottom, then raise it less than a foot and jig it up and down. When he felt a tug, or when he decided it had been down long enough, he hauled in the line, coiling it around a board with an inverted V on either end. A hole carved into the middle of the board enabled him to grip and hold the board with one hand while wrapping the line around it with the other. Occasionally, while Bergie or Minnie rowed, he would troll the line behind the boat.

Herman also fished along the shore with a seine net. At first Olga helped him throw the net out and pull it back in, but as they grew older, Bergie and Minnie took over this job. With the seine they would catch perch, flounder and rock cod. He sold some of his catch to a fish buyer in Egmont or to commercial fishermen who happened to be in the inlet, usually for less than four cents a pound. At other times he sold them to local residents and vacationers, and as the girls got older they would go door to door offering fish for sale. Any unsold catch

Along with their own son and daughter, Anne and Robert Chamberlain brought orphaned children to their Carlson Creek farm, where Bergie and Minnie Solberg were frequent visitors. Photo courtesy of Elizabeth Clode.

THE VALUE OF GOATS

Goat farming was introduced in British Columbia as an experiment in 1919 and within six years there were more than fifteen thousand goats in the province. For the wilderness farmer they proved to be an ideal source of protein from both their milk and their flesh, an aid in keeping brush under control and a relatively odourless source of manure for the garden. Their hides could also be used to make clothing.

Goats have a lifespan of fifteen to twenty-four years and, unlike cattle or sheep, they are browsers, their diet similar to that of deer. They can survive on vines, weeds and wild shrubs such as salmonberry, salal, thimbleberry and elderberry, relieving the farmer of the burden of obtaining a regular supply of hay or grain. Their rich milk is easier on the digestive system and was often preferred in the early part of the twentieth century because goats also have a natural immunity to tuberculosis.

In 1925 the cost of a milking goat ranged from $25 to $50, and from $75 to $150 for a purebred sire. However, since the gestation period for goats is only five months and each doe generally produces two offspring, it did not take long to build up a herd.[9]

became a meal for the family, along with clams and crabs and garden produce, or was used as fertilizer.

"There were few roads then," wrote Nancy Moote. "The sisters would row from Sandy Hook to the government dock at Porpoise Bay, then take a foot trail through the woods to Clayton's store."[10]

"Mother, she used to do all the cooking," Bergie said. "Everybody loved her cooking. Baked her own bread. Made cakes."

William Burt shared her opinion about Olga Solberg. "She was a real lady," he contended, "and an excellent cook. She made delicious rye bread and an excellent fish chowder."

The Solbergs also raised chickens and goats on their farm and it was Minnie and Bergie's job to look after the goats, milking them each morning, cleaning out their shed and tethering them in spots where they could graze on fresh salal and elderberry bushes.

Throughout her life, one of Bergie's favourite treats was *gjetost* (pronounced "yay-toast"), which her mother taught her to make with the whey from a batch of goat cheese. After simmering for hours the whey would develop a sweet, caramel-like taste and solidify into a dark brown cheese. Sliced thin, it would be eaten on flatbread or alone as a dessert.

While the farm enabled the Solbergs to survive without much money, the gardens and animals also attracted wildlife. But according to William Burt, who remembered staying in the unfinished cabin with his mother and sister in the early 1920s, long before the Solberg family took over the pre-emption some animals had already claimed Four Mile Point as their territory.

"In this cabin there was just one bed," he related. "My mother would sleep between my sister and myself. One night we left a ladder up against the building, and two bear cubs went up the ladder and onto the roof. We were panicked, wondering if the sow would get up there and crash through."

A skilled hunter, Herman was not frightened by the bears—although he considered them a nuisance along with cougars and other predators—and with the army rifle he'd brought from Norway, he promptly dispatched any that ventured onto his farm. The girls would then help skin the animal and stretch the hide on the back of a shed to dry. When it was ready for market, he would take the skin to the Union Steamship store and send it to a fur buyer in Vancouver, such as the Hudson's Bay Company, or to Ernest Whitaker, a brother of Sechelt's legendary entrepreneur Herbert Whitaker.

Herman's main defence against marauding wildlife, however, was Bush, a Norwegian elkhound that he acquired after moving to Sechelt. Renowned as a companion to the Vikings, the wolf-faced elkhound is a short, thick-necked breed with a broad chest, a thick coat ranging from dark brown to black and a curled tail. They are fearless dogs and superb trackers, their acute senses of smell and hearing enabling them to pick up the trail of an animal from up to five kilometres away.

As soon as they were capable of keeping up with him, Bergie and Minnie would accompany their father and Bush on hunting treks into the Tetrahedron mountains and up the inlets to Clowhom Falls or Tzoonie Mountain. Herman taught the girls where they could find mountain goats, how to recognize and follow the trail of a deer, how to tell when

The Chamberlains raised goats at their Carlson Creek farm. Photo courtesy of Elizabeth Clode.

Robert Chamberlain rowing at Sechelt in 1926. Photo courtesy of Elizabeth Clode.

the trail had last been used and where a doe had rested with a fawn. They learned to tell the difference between the tracks of a buck, a doe and a fawn, and were soon able to identify those of martin, mink, weasel, otter, raccoon, coyote, bear, bobcat and cougar. They also learned to rub goat fat on themselves and their clothes to mask their human scent.

In 1914 the government placed a bounty on harbour seals, offering payment for each seal snout turned in to the local fishery office. Herman took full advantage of this offer.

"The Solbergs used to keep the inlet free of seals," said William Burt. "Their cabin was always full of seal skins, and there was hardly a seal in the inlet."

George Page, who had a fish-buying station at Egmont, said that in the 1940s Herman, Bergie and Minnie would row to Egmont from Four Mile Point to turn in their seal snouts.

"They got two dollars for each nose," he said, adding that Herman was an unpleasant man. "He'd often arrive really early in the morning and demand breakfast!"

In later years when Page was operating a bulk fuel station in Sechelt, Herman would have him bring his three-ton fuel truck down to the Porpoise Bay wharf and only purchase three dollars' worth of fuel. "And then he wanted a ride from there up to the stores!"

Although Herman could be frightening when he was in a temper and was often grumpy, Bergie idolized her father, and as she grew older, she developed many of his habits, among them a fierce independence and a stubborn determination to do whatever she set her mind to, regardless of obstacles in her way. She also inherited his temper, which became clear when those obstacles became insurmountable.

While Minnie was as at home in the woods as her sister and just as eager to follow after their father, she had developed a greater degree of Olga's gentleness. Her temper flared less often and was milder than that of her father and sister. She was also more at home in the kitchen, learning to cook almost as well as her mother.

Unfortunately, while her husband and daughters revelled in the freedom and adventure of their life at Four Mile Point, Olga grew more and more withdrawn.

"She didn't like it here," said Bergie, "and she liked us to speak Norwegian, not English. She had a terrible time speaking English."

The children with their catches at the Chamberlain farm. Photo courtesy of Elizabeth Clode.

Although there were other Norwegians with whom Olga could occasionally visit—among them Oskar and Albertina Gjerdin, who lived at Doriston—mostly Olga stayed at home. As was the custom in Norway, her role in the family was to take care of the home and to put her husband's comforts ahead of herself or her children. William Burt said this didn't sit well with his father, Charles Burt. The summer that William was thirteen, he and his dad were invited to supper at the Solbergs'. As soon as the men had sat down at the table, Herman began to eat.

"Where's Olga?" asked Charles. "Aren't she and the girls going to sit down?"

"Oh, no," said Herman. "Men eat first."

"Well, Bill and I are leaving if you don't get your wife to sit down," Charles said sternly. "In this country families eat together."

Herman scowled but finally called Olga and the girls to the table, and thereafter in the Burts' presence they shared meals.

The incident, however, did little to shift Herman's attitude toward his wife. In the late 1940s he often visited with the Chambers family on Wharf Road in Sechelt. Ted Chambers was a machinist, and like most Sechelt residents, Herman would have him make a needed part for a rifle or a tool rather than wait for the part to come from a store in the city. If Ted was having a coffee break, his wife, Mildred, would invite Herman to join them. Eventually Mildred discovered that Olga, who sometimes accompanied her husband, had been left waiting in the yard. Thereafter she'd make a special point of extending the invitation to Olga.

By the time Bergie was eight years old, Herman was eligible to apply for citizenship, and knowing how quickly immigration laws could be changed, he wasted no time in doing so. An RCMP report from December 1931 shows that he was recommended for citizenship by the local game warden, T.D. Sutherland, and by Sechelt postmaster Robert S. Hackett. On August 30, 1932, he pledged the Oath of Allegiance to Justice of the Peace Thomas J. Cook, and a month later he received his certificate of naturalization.

On January 27, 1934, having "proved up" his pre-emption by making the necessary improvements to the property as required by the Dominion Lands Act, Herman was granted title to Lot 4679. He was now a Canadian citizen and a property owner and no one could ever send him back to Norway.

GROWING UP

As Bergie and Minnie grew older and were able to handle the boat by themselves, their explorations expanded across the whole Inland Sea. Trips to Sechelt were no longer limited to times when Herman could take them, and they were soon appearing on local doorsteps offering to sell householders a ling cod, a quart of goat's milk or some of Olga's farm produce.

Occasionally the girls would take their mother with them. Alan Wood, who was born and raised in West Sechelt during the 1920s and '30s, often encountered the girls on the water.

"I used to tow them up and down the inlet," he said. "We'd be coming down in the motorboat and see them, so we'd pull alongside and grab their bow rope. One time I was coming down and there were the two girls sitting side-by-side rowing, and their mama was sitting in the back seat. I pulled up alongside, and it was like three squirrels—flip, flip, flip—and they were on board my boat!"

Summer weekends were busy in Sechelt and most of the local children would be at the Trail Bay wharf on Saturday

On excursion days Bergie and Minnie would come to the Union Steamship Company's picnic grounds to watch the games and to stand in line for ice cream and other treats. Photographer unknown, courtesy of Sechelt Community Archives.

and Sunday to watch Union Steamship's excursion boats arrive and discharge hundreds of passengers, mostly employees of companies such as Woodward's department store and Malkin's Foods, which held annual company picnics in Sechelt.

On these days the grounds would be filled with music and activities. Often local children joined in the games organized for the excursionists' children and shared in the free treats available, including tubs of ice cream. Bergie and Minnie would come to watch the games, and while they were too shy to join in, they did stand in line whenever treats were given out.

Both sisters loved ice cream and, when there were no picnics happening at the park, they were still able, once in a very great while, to purchase cones at the Union Steamship store. The late Margaret Hemstreet, eldest daughter of pioneer storekeeper Cedric Clayton, remembered ice cream being available in the summer.

Wharf Road in the 1930s. The Union Steamship picnic grounds on the left is now home to the Legion, while the Whitaker orchard on the right is the site of the Sechelt Animal Hospital. Photographer unknown, courtesy of Sechelt Community Archives.

She recalled, "There was a U-shaped block in the centre of the store. It was closed in the winter, but in the summer they opened it up and stocked it with candy bars and stuff for kids. The ice cream was there. It was quite something to be handed a cone—and it was always one of the long cones, not like nowadays, the little short things. You could probably get vanilla, strawberry and chocolate and nothing else."

Herman, like many other coastal men, was hard pressed to find work during the Depression, but he was able to make some money by helping to build the road from Porpoise Bay to Sechelt, for which he received twenty cents per day. William Burt remembered walking out to Gray Creek in 1933 and seeing Herman with a wheelbarrow, pick and shovel, constructing a road for the Irving family who owned a large retreat at

Dr. Richard Elvin hired Herman Solberg to do odd jobs on his West Porpoise Bay property. Later the Solbergs used the Elvin driveway to access their boats and a raft full of junk. Photo courtesy of Cavin Crawford and Sechelt Community Archives.

Tranquility Bay in Tuwanek. Much of the work assigned to him and other road workers was digging ditches and putting in drainage systems which, according to a Public Works Report for 1936–37, "lent itself better to hand-labour, especially local relief-work."[11]

Herman also continued to work as a handyman. Dr. Richard Elvin, who had a summer home on West Porpoise Bay, often hired him to cut firewood or do other chores around the property.

"He helped build the cottage that's still there," said Elvin's son, who was also named Richard. "He was good friends with my dad, who looked after the Solbergs' medical needs."

Often Herman worked for Charles Jordan, who had a sawmill next to the Elvin property.

"Herman was a big man with big hands and a broad back," said Faith (Elvin) Darnbrought. "He used to help Mr. Jordan roll the logs onto the cutter to saw them. And he helped my father roll logs three to four feet in diameter up our embankment to stop it from eroding."

In the fall of 1935, when they were twelve and thirteen years old, Bergie and Minnie set off on a hunting trip of their own. Bergie toted her father's .38-55 Winchester rifle as they followed a game trail roughly paralleling Gray Creek and cut through old logging slashes now covered in wild grasses and an abundance of new, leafy shrubs such as salmonberry, thimbleberry and wild currants, on which deer love to browse. The slashes were also filled with stumps and boulders and unexpected depressions, often covered over by decaying limbs that could collapse when stepped on. The girls risked serious injury from inadvertently stumbling into one of these holes, tripping over limbs or slipping on gravel loosened by uprooted trees and erosion. But they were unharmed when they returned to Four Mile Point many hours later and presented their family with a large buck.

Although it was not Herman's way to praise his daughters, in 1975 the late Rhody Lake quoted him in a *Vancouver Sun* feature article, "Woman of the Woods," as saying proudly that when Bergie was about twelve she "shot a big buck right through the heart. That was about two miles back in the hills."[12]

By this time Minnie and Bergie were travelling up and down the inlets with ease, but being aware of the dangers they faced, they almost always carried a tarp on their journeys. When the sea became too rough to travel safely, they'd row to the nearest shore, build a small shelter with the tarp and remain there, often overnight, until it was safe to proceed.

In 1935 Herman secured a thirty-two-kilometre trapline that extended from "the mouth of Carlson Creek on the west side of Sechelt Inlet, thence south along shoreline of said inlet to and round the south end, and north along the east side to and along Gray Creek, including all tributaries of said creek and Tannis Lake but not including any private property or Indian Reserve."[13]

"He caught a bunch of mink in live traps," Bergie said when asked about her father's trapping. "He caught them in the fall and we kept them in nice little cages. They got nice and shiny after we fed them all this fish. He kept them till the season was to get rid of them. Then he'd take them to the fur buyer."

That first winter Herman's total recorded catch was six mink, two weasels and one wildcat.

The dance pavilion on the boulevard hosted movies, roller skating and dances. Bergie and Minnie were usually content to sit on the sidelines to listen and watch. Photo c. 1937 by Harry Winn, courtesy of Vancouver City Archives.

Although they never had much money, the 1930s and 1940s were good years for the Solbergs. They were secure in their home at Four Mile Point, far enough away from civilization to do what they pleased, yet close enough to obtain the things they needed without too much trouble.

George Page, who fished the inlets with his father during these years, remembers fishing Porpoise Bay for herring.

"When we were coming from Egmont to Porpoise Bay," he said, "the Solbergs' was the only light you could see on the inlet."

As Bergie and Minnie grew older they began to attend more social activities in Sechelt. One of their favourite pastimes was to watch the films that Pacific Mobile Movies brought to the Union Steamship's dance pavilion next to the tea house. The sixteen-

Though badly damaged, this is the only existing photo of the Solberg family. From left to right: Minnie, Olga, Herman and Bergie. Date and place unknown. Photo courtesy of Elizabeth Clode.

millimetre reels would often arrive damaged or broken, and the first time they were shown there were many stops for repairs. For this reason Rudy Crucil, who also attended these movies, would never attend the first run of a show. The first movie he remembered watching was a Tom Mix western. Joan O'Shea recalled that even in the late 1940s the theatre was very rustic.

"It had wooden benches," she said, "and sometimes a dog would walk in."

The dance pavilion also became a roller skating rink three times a week and although Bergie and Minnie didn't skate, they liked to listen to the music from the Wurlitzer and watch the young people whirl about on rubber-wheeled skates. Alan Wood, who was often there, said the event sometimes got rough, but according to Dorothy Robilliard, it could also lead to romance.

"That's where I met my husband," she said. "He was logging at Halfmoon Bay where Mr. Tait had a taxi. He brought these young loggers down every Friday night to roller skate."

Surrounded by forest as they were at Four Mile Point, the Solbergs, like most Sunshine Coast residents, were always concerned about fire. The summer of 1938 was especially hot, and although the woods were not closed to logging, those who continued to work were on their guard, watching for friction sparks that could come from cables running along the ground, from boiler fires or simply from two dislodged rocks striking each other. As careful as the logging operators were, however, they were unable to prevent a fire that broke out at the De Long Brothers logging operation on Salmon Inlet, close enough to Herman's trapping and hunting territory to worry him. By the time it was contained, 762,000 metres of cut timber were destroyed, but Herman's trapline was still intact.

LADY LOGGER

Herman was forty-eight at the start of World War II and not required to enlist, but he was able to capitalize on the increased demand for dogfish. Because the oil produced from their livers was used on airplane wings, the price for these fish rose steadily after 1939. Bergie and Minnie, who were now seventeen and eighteen years old, often joined their father fishing, and as in previous years sold their dogfish to packers and their salmon and bottom fish to local residents. At other times they helped Herman with his trapline, which throughout the 1940s provided a steady supply of mink, bear, otter, raccoon, weasel, lynx and cougar pelts.

Timber was also much in demand during the war, and many of those who stayed behind worked in the woods. Soon there were more logging jobs than there were men to fill them, and as in other industries, women were employed in their place. Bergie was hired by the Osborne Logging Company Ltd. to work at their Halfmoon Bay camp.

An Osborne Logging Company truck, fully loaded. Date and place unknown. Photo courtesy of Margaret Pearson and Sechelt Community Archives.

WHISTLEPUNKS

In the early high-lead logging process, a sturdy tree was limbed and topped, anchored to nearby stumps with guy wires, then rigged as a spar with blocks and tackle and cables that were connected to a winch and extended to the boundaries of the cut area, which could be up to two kilometres away.

A wire cable that was attached to one of the high-lead wires was fastened around a log by either the chokerman or the rigging slinger, who then shouted a command to the whistlepunk. Using a hand-held signal box that was connected by metres of electric cable to a whistle on the yarding machine, the whistlepunk relayed the command. Resembling a crude spring-loaded rectangular castanet, the signal box brought two contacts together when squeezed and caused the whistle to blow. When released it would spring apart, break the contact and stop the whistle. The number of times that the wires touched the contacts would determine the number of whistles, and each combination gave the yarder operator a different message such as "haul in" or "haul back" or "stop."

"I was a whistlepunk," she recalled, adding, after a self-conscious giggle, "I don't know why they called them that."

In 1941 Ted Osborne harvested sixteen million board feet of timber using a high-lead system, which had been developed

An Osborne Logging Company truck and a slash hill. As a whistlepunk, Bergie had to scramble over limbs and stumps, avoid hidden holes and watch for powerful cables and logs whipping above her head. Photo courtesy of Margaret Pearson and Sechelt Community Archives.

in the first decade of the twentieth century with wooden spar trees. Logs were yarded to a landing close to where they were cut, then trucked along a network of roads Osborne had built from the mouth of Carlson Creek, where it emptied into the west side of Sechelt Inlet, to a second landing at Halfmoon Bay on Georgia Strait. There they were scaled and "dumped" into the water.

The rigging slinger in charge of Osborne's rigging crew was Thomas (Tom) Hugh Parish, one of the most renowned high riggers on the Sunshine Coast. He had met Bergie in 1938 when she appeared at the logging camp selling fish, and

Tom Parish trained Bergie as a whistlepunk and treated her, as he did everyone, with a gentle respect. 1960s photo by Harold Swanson, courtesy of Bea Swanson and Sechelt Community Archives.

when she eventually went to work for Osborne, Parish trained her as a whistlepunk.

After showing her how to operate the signal box, Parish explained the importance of sending the correct signal, stressing that a mix-up could bring the yarding operation to a standstill or, even worse, cause a fatal accident by moving a log before everyone was out of the way. No matter how difficult the terrain, it was critical that she stay close enough to the chokerman and the high rigger to hear the message they wanted her to send to the yarder.

In those first days Bergie often became flustered, especially when, having sent the signal, she missed hearing the whistle and worried that she had not made a proper connection. At those times she would have to fight the urge to send the signal again, knowing that if she did, the wrong message would go out to the yarder. When some of the loggers became impatient and yelled at her, she became even more agitated and occasionally came close to tears. But Parish had a gentle way of talking that always calmed her down and helped her focus on the job that had to be done.

"Bergie was quiet. And strong," he said, adding that she was also a hard worker.

Herman had built a rowboat for Bergie and every morning she would row across the inlet from Four Mile Point to Carlson Creek, then hike up to the cut. No matter how cold the weather was, she refused to wear gloves because they made it harder to handle the signal box. And because rain gear impaired her ability to move about the slash, she relied instead on wool sweaters and a wide-brimmed hat. Occasionally one of the crew would build a fire so she could get warm, but Bergie would never stop to build one for herself.

Minnie also found work in logging camps, often as a whistlepunk. However, because she was shyer than Bergie and liked to stay closer to the wilderness areas, she preferred the job of looking after logging camps while the crew was on holidays.

Although Herman and Olga must have been concerned about their relatives in Norway when Hitler's army invaded that country in 1940, the war in Europe did not drastically change their lives. The food and other supplies that were rationed were not things that they could afford anyway, and they had no sons to send off to fight. However, they were disturbed when the Japanese families on the coast were sent to internment camps. Bergie and Minnie had played with the Konishi children in Sechelt, and Herman had purchased produce and other supplies from the Takais, Maedas, and Hatashita family stores in Egmont and had sold fish to their fish-buying stations.

In August 1945 Ted Osborne sold his Halfmoon Bay logging operation to Westminster Shook Mills Ltd.[14] and turned his attention to developing his camp at Narrows Inlet. Since there was already a whistlepunk at the Narrows Camp, Bergie had to look for work elsewhere. By this time men were demobilizing from the armed forces, and jobs for women were fast disappearing. Over the next five years she worked as a whistlepunk, set chokers or climbed spar trees for various outfits, including John Bosch's camp at Middle Point. These jobs enabled her to continue hunting and exploring the wilderness areas of Sechelt, Narrows and Salmon inlets until she came to know the back trails and abandoned routes to old logging sites better than most people knew the streets of their hometowns. Sometimes she had a boat with a motor and was able to travel to and from camp in a matter of hours, but often, when she had no gas or her boat motor wasn't working, she would row.

One day in the fall of 1949, Bergie was with her parents at Four Mile Point when she heard someone calling from across the inlet. Without hesitating, she went to her boat and motored across to the old Osborne landing where two men were waiting, one suffering from a severe head injury. Robert Lemieux had been working several kilometres inland for Russ Boise Logging.

He and his co-worker, Jerry, had taken one of the company trucks—an old army vehicle with a right-hand drive—down to pick up some cable. The route was steep with lots of hairpin bends near the bottom.

"I geared down," said Lemieux, "but I didn't have any brakes. The truck bounced up so we were airborne and slammed into a pine tree on the corner. I got hit in the face with a post that came right through the window."

His friend patched him up as best he could, and they walked over a kilometre down to the beach.

"Bergie picked us up and took us to the doctor at Porpoise Bay. It was Dr. McColl, who had an office in a Union Estates building that stood where the Beach House complex is now."

It was Lemieux's first introduction to Bergie, but he came to know her well a year later when they were both working for Gus Crucil's logging company. The Crucil booming ground was located on the Sechelt Inlet waterfront between the lower end of Dusty Road and Kontiki Road.

"She came every morning in a little boat with an inboard motor," said Lemieux, who was Crucil's yarding machine operator. "She was seldom late, and she seldom missed work, although sometimes she forgot to get gas the night before and had to row over."

From the booming ground the crew would travel to the logging site in a "crummy" made from a converted pick-up truck with a high canopy. Secured on either side were wooden benches for the workers to sit on.

"Bergie was as strong as many of the men," Lemieux related. "But it wasn't so much strength as her willingness to get in there. She picked things up very quickly."

Bergie was proud of her job as a logger and considered herself just one of the guys. Occasionally, however, the real guys would banter with her.

"Johnny Whyte," remembered Lemieux, "used to love to tease Bergie. He'd grab her about mid-thigh and she would giggle her head off. She never indicated that she was angry about it. She could have cold-cocked him if she wanted. Others might try to tease her like that, but they didn't get the same reaction. They didn't touch her like Johnny did."

According to Egmont fisherman William "Billy" Griffith, once when Bergie was travelling up to the woods in a logging truck, one of the loggers tried to snuggle up and get a kiss from her.

"She squawked and threw him out of the truck," said Griffith, "and he broke his arm when he landed! Served him right for being so rough with her."

Although she worked hard at logging, Bergie continued to enjoy town events, especially when Minnie was with her. At the end of the war, Gordon West had re-established Pacific Motion Pictures and was once again bringing movies to Gibsons, Pender Harbour and the Pavilion in Sechelt, showing films like *The Gentleman from Arizona* and *So Goes My Love*. The sisters attended whenever they could, and they also went to the dances held in the Legion Hall and the Pavilion. It was at one of these dances that the late Ed Laidlaw, who came to the Sunshine Coast in 1947, first came to know them.

"Bergie and her sister would be sitting on the side, just enjoying the music, though a few loggers would try to get them up to dance."

Bergie (left) and Minnie (right) lived separate lives but often travelled together to the PNE or to the Calgary stampede to hear their favourite singer, Wilf Carter. Photo c. 1976, courtesy of Faye McCourt and Sechelt Community Archives.

Every year, according to Cavin Crawford, Bergie would show up at his grandfather's Porpoise Bay boathouse, change and go for a swim. Then she'd board the bus for the PNE in Vancouver. Photo courtesy of Cavin Crawford.

Most of the dances the girls went to featured country and western music, which Bergie loved, especially the songs of Hank Snow and Wilf Carter. So great was their love for Carter that in the 1970s, when he became a Calgary Stampede marshal, Bergie and Minnie made several trips to the stampede just to see and hear him sing.

They also went to the musical events at the Pacific National Exhibition in Vancouver and always dressed up for these visits.

"They wore cowboy shirts with embroidery, always purple or blue, I think," said Joan O'Shea. "They loved them."

"At the end of August Bergie always wanted to go to the PNE," said Cavin Crawford, a grandson of Dr. Richard Elvin, "but they wouldn't let her on the bus unless she had a bath. So she'd go into my grandfather's boathouse and change into a bathing suit and go for a swim, then go to the PNE and come back with a new purple cowboy hat with a whistle on it."

Bergie learned to sing the Snow and Carter songs she heard on the radio and even learned how to strum a guitar and yodel.

"We would swim together," said Dr. Elvin's son, Richard, "then she'd come up for dinner. She'd have a few glasses of wine and she'd sing and yodel all the Wilf Carter songs."

In later years, Wendy Young asked Bergie who taught her to yodel. "Bergie said whenever her dad was mad at her, she would climb a mountain and just sit there and scream, and the scream would come back. She thought that was quite funny." One day Wendy asked for a demonstration, "and she let rip. She was excellent! Excellent." Then Bergie suggested that Wendy try it herself. "She laughed because I sounded awful and suggested that maybe I should go up the mountain and practise."

Few people, however, learned of Bergie's talent, and she and Minnie continued to sit on the sidelines at dances, unless there was a square dance where everyone joined in.

To many people the girls, now in their early twenties, were oddities.

"They'd put on a skirt and wear a big hat to the dances," said Jean Wood.

Others remembered that the girls' dresses were suited more to their mother's era, and instead of nylons they wore heavy lisle stockings and sturdy walking shoes.

"They always stood out," said Faye Hansen, who was one of Alan Wood's sisters.

Osborne Logging operation. During World War II Bergie got her first job working as a whistlepunk for the Osborne Logging Company at their Halfmoon Bay camp. Photo courtesy of Margaret Pearson and Sechelt Community Archives.

One reason for this was that Minnie and Bergie lacked basic social skills. Although Olga Solberg was well mannered, she seemed to have decided that such graces were of little use to girls raised in the bush. Or perhaps her own spirit was so broken she did not have the heart to try to turn her two wild daughters into young ladies. In the end, according to several townspeople, the social skills the girls did acquire were largely due to the efforts of Eric Knutson, a kind old Norwegian shoemaker. Knutson lived on Trident Avenue and owned a shoemaking and repair shop, where he specialized in making good quality shoes and logging boots to order. He was a bachelor, and when the girls could find no work in the logging industry, he would sometimes hire them to help him around the house.

"Bergie and Minnie were in their twenties then," said Faye Hansen, adding that Knutson "didn't have much use for their old man."

"Eric Knutson got the girls to clean up and take better care of themselves," said Dean Robilliard, who grew up near Porpoise Bay.

Occasionally the wives of Bergie's coworkers tried to get the girls to dress differently.

"We used to go up to the Wakefield," said Robert Lemieux. "It was the only source of liquor at that time. Once Bergie and Minnie came up there and we talked them into going to a dance."

His wife, Kaye, nodded. "They came to our house and I helped them put on lipstick and combed their hair. I told Bergie to leave her hat at home, but all evening it bothered her. She kept wiping her lips with the back of her hand and saying, 'Oh, my hat!' She obviously felt very uncomfortable about it."

At some point during the 1940s a few local residents started calling Bergie "Myrtle," because it sounded cute with "Minnie," and soon many people accepted "Myrtle" as Bergie's real name. One day Joan O'Shea and a friend were walking up to the Union Steamship store just as Bergie and Minnie were leaving. They stopped to talk, and when they parted, the girls said, "Bye, Minnie. Bye, Myrtle."

Bruce Crowston, who was standing nearby, was not pleased. "Do you know her name is not Myrtle?" he asked. "Her name is Bergliot, and I don't think it's very nice for people to make a joke of her name."

Joan and her friend returned home and recounted the incident to their parents. "Dad and Mom were surprised because they didn't know that her name was Bergliot," said Joan. "They thought it was Myrtle because that's all anyone in town ever called her." From then on, their father insisted that they call Bergie by her proper name.

AWAY FROM HOME AND ALL ALONE

In 1952 Bergie was hired as a camp watcher for Universal Timber Products at Sechelt Creek near the head of Salmon Inlet. A truck logging show, it was owned and operated by the Horace Johnson family, who had been logging at Sechelt Creek for almost ten years and were in the process of moving their camp to Port Mellon.

"Not including fallers," said Norm Johnson, "we regularly hired about ten men."

Norm and his brothers worked as loggers, setting chokers and rigging spars. Their sister helped their father in the office, which was located on the beach at Sechelt Creek—and was still standing there at the time of writing.

"Our town office was on the beach at Twin Creeks in Gibsons," Norm said.

It took time to move a logging operation, and while the Johnsons were establishing the camp at Port Mellon, they needed someone to watch the Sechelt Creek site to ensure that the valuable equipment there was not stolen or vandalized before they could come back for it. When Bergie heard that the Johnsons were looking for someone to watch their camp, she decided it was the opportunity she needed to branch out on her own. She was now twenty-nine years old and she was outgrowing the little family cabin at Four Mile Point. By this time she had acquired a small herd of goats, chickens and some draft horses and, having perfected her father's talent for finding free items, her collection of odds and ends rivalled his.

"My dad asked how much she wanted to come and watch camp," related Norm Johnson. "She had all these animals she wanted to bring up, and she decided three hundred dollars a month was what she wanted. Everything was done more or less by a handshake."

According to Norm, there were ten buildings at Sechelt Creek: three that had been homes for family members, one office and six smaller buildings used as shops and houses for the crew. For Bergie it was paradise. She had all of the backcountry to hunt and explore, great fishing in the creek and on the saltchuck and plenty of space for her animals. And she had neighbours at Clowhom Falls, just seven kilometres up the inlet from the Universal camp.

Since the early 1930s Effie and Godfriedus "Kim" Kym had been living at Clowhom as caretakers of a private fishing lodge owned by American lumberman Frederick W. Leadbetter's company, Columbia Steamship Company Inc. In 1927 Leadbetter's Columbia River Paper Company had purchased the Howe Sound Pulp and Paper Company at Port Mellon. Effie, who had worked as a chokerman and a cook for her family's logging operation near Vancouver Island, developed a special kinship with Bergie and they soon became close friends.

Art and Gwen Asseltine also lived at Clowhom Falls along with their neighbours, William "Bill" Schott and family. Both men were operators of the Clowhom power station, a 4,000-horsepower hydro-electric generating station that had been built there by the BC Power Commission in 1950. The families lived in two company houses beside the huge concrete Clowhom Dam, just a short trail length away from Kim and Effie's home. Gwen's sister Betty Laidlaw and her husband, Ed, often visited the Asseltines at Clowhom and later came to live there themselves.

"Kim and Effie took Bergie under their wing," said Betty. "They would have her up there for dinner quite often."

Faye Hansen also remembered travelling up the inlet to visit the Schotts and Asseltines. "Bergie would row over from Sechelt Creek," she said. "We'd have a good dinner and Bergie would come. She was good company then. Sometimes she'd get lonely or homesick at night and she'd go home to Sechelt."

Betty Laidlaw remembered a New Year's party at Clowhom. "The fellows decided to get Bergie drunk, much to the disapproval of us women. They began feeding her drinks. She matched them drink for drink, but while the men were doing little more than drinking, Bergie was also eating everything in sight—oranges, nuts, sausage rolls. She was giggling and laughing with the fellows, but she didn't get drunk by any means."

The next day Bergie came to dinner at Kim and Effie's, and they asked how she was and how she had made out on her way home the previous evening.

At a 1957 Clowhom Falls New Year's party, Bergie matched the men drink for drink, then rowed home to Sechelt Creek. "The boat seemed to be going this way and that," she remarked later. "It took twice as long to get there." Photo courtesy of Faye Hansen.

"Fine," she replied, "but it was funny. That boat seemed to be going this way and that. It took twice as long to get there."

Back at Four Mile Point, Herman was busy building a new boat, this time a thirty-six-foot double-ender fishing vessel.

"He was going to fish with it in the Fraser River," said Ray Stockwell, whose father, Herb Stockwell, cut the lumber Herman needed to build the boat. "But by the time he got it built, he was too old, and he had to get a special licence by this time to fish."

Herman installed a sixteen-horsepower Vivian engine in the boat. When it didn't run fast enough for him, he tore the cams off and repinned them at different angles, but the engine still turned at the same speed. Eventually he installed a twenty-horsepower Easthope engine, and for many years he used the boat as his main mode of transportation on the inlet. Although he registered the vessel as the *Fjeld*, people living on and around the inlet nicknamed it the "Bismarck."

Although Herman chose *Fjeld* as the name for the thirty-six-foot double-ender he built to go fishing on the Fraser River, folks around the inlet called it the *Bismarck*. Photo courtesy of Oddvin Vedo, oddvinvedo.wordpress.com.

Occasionally, Herman did take time from his boat building to help Bergie out at Sechelt Creek, but not because he was interested in logging.

To meet the challenge of providing jobs for returning soldiers after World War II, the governments of BC and Canada began subsidizing, or "grubstaking," prospectors in the hope that they would find new ore bodies. As a result of the publicity this generated, Herman had developed an obsession for gold and dreamed of finding a motherlode. Visiting Sechelt Creek gave him an opportunity to investigate Alexander Donaldson's abandoned mine.

"Oh, sure," Bergie said when asked about the mine. "I went up top and got some pretty stones out of that place. I had a horse that time and I rode up. Then I let the horse go and he run all the way back home. You just walk and then turn to the left. I had to walk through the bush. That's a tunnel up there. I've never been in the tunnel, but I've looked at it. It goes kind of in. It's not down. I took pictures of it. Then I took pictures of the nice blue lakes on top."

MINING MOUNT DONALDSON

In 1874 Alexander Donaldson, having discovered an outcrop of copper at the 945-metre level of what is now Mount Donaldson, staked six claims in the name of his newly formed Howe Sound Copper and Silver Mine Company and sank a nine-metre test tunnel. Government mining engineer R.B. Harvey, who inspected the mine in June 1877, was enthusiastic about the find, reporting, "It is the richest ore of this character I have ever seen on this Coast or in England. I firmly believe that the lode will, at a greater depth from the surface, prove to be richer in silver than in copper …"[15]

Although the mine was just four kilometres from Salmon Inlet, the only way to get to it was via an eleven-kilometre horse trail from the inlet up Sechelt Creek to its confluence with Slippery Creek. From there, the miners packed their equipment up Slippery Creek canyon and over a bald granite peak to the mine site. No attempt was made to build a road, but the company carried out enough ore on pack animals for a small shipment to a smelter at Swansea, Wales. The results were never made public and by 1883 the mine was shut down.

A mid-1920s rise in the price of copper brought prospectors back to Mount Donaldson, and the old pack trail from Salmon Inlet was widened so that heavy equipment could be brought in. Two of Donaldson's old claims became part of a four-hundred-acre site belonging to a new company, Pacific Copper Mines Ltd., and four million shares were offered to the public at twenty-five cents each. A mining camp was constructed near the old mine workings, 1,370 metres above sea level, but high-grade ore was never found. When a Radiore survey also proved disappointing, Pacific Copper retrieved its equipment from the mountaintop and began acquiring mining properties elsewhere.

Eventually, having found no obvious evidence of silver or gold and faced with the difficulties of retrieving the copper ore, the Solbergs decided Mount Donaldson was not going to provide them with the fortune they were seeking. Many years later a far different site would capture their attention and almost cost Bergie her life.

Although Universal Timber Products had ceased logging, Bill Bestwick's Misery Creek Logging Company started a new operation in 1952 across the inlet from Sechelt Creek.

"Bergie lived in a camp across the bay from us," Bestwick said, "and she worked in the woods for us one summer as a whistlepunk."

Bestwick's camp included a cookhouse and bunkhouses.

"I had the first electric, rubber-tired arch that pulled the trees to the tidewater," he boasted. "A LeTourneau electric arch. The first one on the whole coast. I heard about it and I went down to

While camp watching for Universal Timber in the 1950s, Bergie also worked for Bill Bestwick at Misery Creek. "If anyone came to the dock," said the late Ed Laidlaw, "she would drop what she was doing, run down the mountain, hop in her boat and row over to see who it was." Photo courtesy of Bill Bestwick.

LeTourneau's in Longview, Texas. They had machines that were kind of like it, but they didn't have the arch part. Basically, this was a machine they were building for other purposes, and they just added an arch onto it. It was kind of like a spar and a winch with a cable on it to pull the logs up and hold them. We dragged the trees into a landing with a gas donkey, then we made up a turn of maybe ten trees, depending on their size, and dragged them down the road with this electric arch."

Like her other employers, Bestwick found that Bergie worked better than some of the men he hired.

"She was quite a character. She lived by herself, had a little boat and hunted. Very independent. An outdoor, rugged type of person. Done anything a man could do or would try to do, liking hunting, fishing and working. She wasn't out of place. She had a big rowboat with a little Briggs motor in it."

Bestwick also maintained that the men in camp respected Bergie. Although they'd joke among themselves about who was going to take her out, they didn't make such comments in her hearing. "If they did get smart with her, she'd tell them where they could go."

Ed Laidlaw said that Bergie enjoyed working at Misery Creek. "She liked it because they were working on the hillside and she could look down on Sechelt Creek. If anyone came up to her dock, she'd drop what she was doing, run down the mountain, hop into her boat and head over to see who it was and what they wanted. Art and I came up to the dock one day and a few moments later Bergie arrived in her boat, puffing and panting. She'd run all the way down because she'd seen us."

Minnie also worked as a whistlepunk and as a camp watchperson for logging operations along Sechelt and Narrows inlets. In 1951 she was living and working as a farmhand at the Jack Gibb farm in Roberts Creek. Gibb's nephew, David Birdsall, was twelve at the time and spent part of two summers with his uncle.

"Minnie had a room at the entrance to the farmhouse so that she could get in and out at all hours without disturbing the family," Birdsall wrote. "Her room was hardly the epitome of tidiness."

"She was certainly capable of doing many things around the farm," he added. "She managed the cows and chickens well and I suppose she occasionally had a bath!"

One day after Gibb had butchered a cow, Minnie asked for permission to collect the blood for "blood pancakes."

It wasn't long, however, before Minnie was back working in logging camps along the inlets.

According to local legend, one day she developed severe stomach cramps and went to see Dr. McColl in his new offices above the Bank of Montreal in Sechelt. It turned out that the stomach cramps were labour pains and within hours she had given birth to a baby girl. There is no indication that Minnie wanted to keep the baby, which was immediately given up for adoption, and no one knew who had fathered the child. However, in a 2004 interview Wendell Welander, who once owned Coast Western Airlines, recalled being present when Minnie remarked to a reporter, "This nice logger stopped in one day for coffee and I got pregnant!"

In 1957 Joan O'Shea shared a room at St. Mary's Hospital at Garden Bay with Minnie, who was recovering from the birth of her second daughter.

"I guess I made it come early," Minnie told O'Shea. "Yesterday I was bringing a bear down and I was tired. I guess now I shouldn't have carried that bear down by myself."

As with the first one, this child was also given up for adoption, but according to Joan, Minnie did not appear very happy about it. "Usually both girls laughed easily. And Minnie still did that, but not the same. She was just less loud, less laughing. It was more of a habit. I think she wanted to go home."

When her third and final child, a boy, was born on May 12, 1963, Minnie was partnered with a prawn fisherman named Henry Dray. Neither parent, however, wanted to keep the child. Henry paid for the delivery and told Dr. Eric Paetkau, "I'll be

Minnie Solberg at the former Bear Bay Logging camp at Deserted Bay. When Jackson Brothers Logging bought the camp, they found Minnie and Henry Dray ensconced as caretakers. Photo c. 1965, courtesy of Pete Jackson and Sechelt Community Archives.

back at the end of the season, Doc. If Minnie's well enough to fly, send her out by plane."

According to Paetkau, Henry Dray was "well-spoken and looked like an English gentleman."

Born in Saskatchewan in 1916, Henry was married in 1936 and moved to British Columbia with his then-wife, Ivy. In 1941 he joined the navy and trained as an engineer, serving until 1945. After mustering out of the services, he purchased a fishing boat, the *Argyle*, and began fishing up and down the coast.

"Henry once had a serious accident on his boat," said Faye Hansen. "He was down the coast fishing and he reached over a machine and his shirt got caught. It pulled him into the mechanism. He was laid up for a long time."

Henry was also an inventor. In 1964 he secured a patent for his "Echo Distance Measuring Systems," a depth-finder that he used on his fishing boat.

Minnie obtained her own commercial fishing licence in 1960 so she could crew on fishing boats. When in 1964 she applied for her fourth licence, Henry Dray signed an affidavit stating, "I have known [Minnie Solberg] to be a resident of Sechelt over the past five years."

In 1972 Minnie watched the controlled burning of buildings at the closing of a Jackson Brothers Camp in Jervis Inlet where she had been the watchperson. Photographer unknown, courtesy of Pete Jackson and Sechelt Community Archives.

Between fishing trips the couple camp-watched for various logging companies up and down the coast. In 1966 when Jackson Brothers Logging bought an outfit at Deserted Bay on Jervis Inlet, they found Minnie and Henry already ensconced there as caretakers for the Bear Bay Logging company. They had a house and garden and maintained that residence even after the camp shut down in 1972.

"They had a fantastic place," said Dr. Paetkau, who went on a hunting trip to Deserted Bay during the 1960s. "An old house, bigger than the shack at Porpoise Bay, and they had rabbits and ducks. I always thought it looked like a hobbit farm—the way the animals had burrowed under these big cedar roots."

Henry had built a huge water wheel on site. It produced electricity and powered a small television, which both Minnie and Bergie—whenever she visited them—loved to watch.

Although Henry cared a great deal for Minnie, they were not always on the best of terms. In the early 1960s Henry would anchor the *Argyle* in Porpoise Bay in front of the Elvin residence. Cavin Crawford remembered that on several occasions Minnie rowed ashore in the middle of the night and complained tearfully to his mother that Henry had gotten drunk and beat her up. But Minnie wasn't always the injured party in their battles. Once when Dr. Paetkau visited the Deserted Bay camp, he was told that the police were on their way to pick up Minnie because Henry was charging her with assault. When the police arrived, Henry said, "She hit me with a two-by-four."

"I did not," Minnie protested.

"You did too!" Henry insisted, and again Minnie said, "I did not!"

Finally the police officer turned to Minnie and asked, "What *did* you do?"

"I hit him with a two-by-six," Minnie responded.

Everyone laughed at that, even Henry, who turned to the police officer and said, "Okay, forget it. I'm not charging her."[16]

Rod Lizee, a pilot for Tyee Airways, which was owned and operated by Al Campbell, said that Minnie would often hang around the Tyee office in Sechelt.

"The boss would tell me to fly her into camp and not charge her," he said. "We'd go out to the float and she'd ask me to move the airplane back because she had nine boxes to load!"

The company's pilot shack was located near the airplanes, and it was not unusual for Minnie to walk in on the crew, whether they were eating or not.

"She'd walk in, take the phone without asking, dial a number and do her business, then walk out again."

Sometimes when Lizee flew supplies into Deserted Bay, Minnie was absent.

"I'd ask her husband where she was and he'd say she was up the mountain hunting, and he didn't know when she'd be back—maybe in two or three days."

Minnie also had a hospitable side and once brought Lizee in to have a piece of pie.

"I wasn't sure about that," he said, "because her mode of dress was questionable. But she kept her house pretty clean, so I felt okay about it."

"It used to be fun going up there," said Ray Stockwell, who frequently visited Henry and Minnie at Deserted Bay when his children were young. "They just loved us to come and they'd treat us so good. Spend all their time with the kids, show them all their animals. Give us vegetables and fruit and wine—all this stuff to bring home. We didn't really bring very much for them, but boy, they were sure happy to see us come. I think they made a really good impression on my kids."

Henry Dray also raised bees, and once when his bees had died from an unknown ailment, the late Iris Griffith gave him a queen so he could start a new hive. Her husband, William,

Tyee Airways airplane at Porpoise Bay Wharf. Although they occasionally used the airline for transportation, Bergie and Minnie also used the airline offices as a place to make phone calls and to park their father while they did business in town. Photo 1966 by the *Peninsula Times*, courtesy of the Alsgard family and Sechelt Community Archives.

who knew Henry as "Harry," remembered how Dray's bees once swarmed up a tree, settling so high up that he couldn't get up there to recapture them.

"Are they gone for good?" Minnie asked.

"That's right."

"You can't get them back at all?"

"Nope," Henry replied, whereupon Minnie went inside for her shotgun.

"She blew the swarm apart with her gun!" Griffith marvelled.

The late Dr. Alan Swan also used to visit Deserted Bay, but said he never went hunting with Minnie.

"Her husband warned me never to go hunting with her because you could never depend on her coming back at a certain time, or to rendezvous at certain times."

While Minnie wasn't a dependable hunting guide, Dr. Swan maintained that she was a hard worker and did much of the work around the place.

"He had a terrible heart, Henry did," said Dr. Swan. "He had been a commercial fisherman who had finally become so helpless with heart disease and cardiovascular disease that he had bypasses everywhere."

Living in Jervis Inlet didn't stop Minnie from going to town, or from visiting her parents as often as she could.

"Sometimes she rowed from Deserted Bay to Egmont," said Pete Jackson. "She had a little Boston Whaler, twelve feet long. That type of boat has a point on either end. She always had a gun and a dog and a piece of canvas for making a tent on the beach. If she didn't make it, she'd pull up on a beach and spend the night."

PARTINGS

Olga's health began declining when she was in her late fifties. By 1960 high blood pressure and several small strokes had confined her to a wheelchair, and she was unable to care for herself. It was around this time that a representative from a real estate development company, Capilano Highlands Ltd., asked Herman if he wanted to sell the Four Mile Point property. While he would have spurned any such offer a few years earlier, Olga's failing health and the need to have her closer to medical care caused him to consider it. However, the most important factor in his decision to sell was the recent publication of stories in several newspapers about an American prospector who was killed while searching for Slumach's Lost Creek gold mine in the mountains near Pitt River.

It is possible that Herman first read about this mine in "Hoodoo Gold," an article by Clyde Gilmour that was featured in the magazine section of the January 18, 1947, *Vancouver Daily Province.*

SLUMACH'S GOLD

According to a mixture of legend, newspaper reports and eye-witness accounts, around 1890 gold was discovered by a Coquitlam Native man named Slumach. It was said that he visited a New Westminster store where he sold a shot bag half-filled with gold nuggets that he claimed he had obtained from the mountainous wilderness above Pitt River. However, on January 16, 1891, Slumach was hanged in New Westminster for the murder of a Port Douglas Native, Louie Bee. Just before he was executed he supposedly uttered a curse: "*Nika memloose, mine memloose,*" which meant, "When I die, mine dies."[17]

The gold legend was given more credibility a few months after Slumach's hanging when American prospector John Jackson ventured into the Pitt Lake Mountain Range in search of the source of the gold. He returned weeks later with a sack of nuggets that eventually netted him ten thousand dollars, but his health was ruined by the hardships he'd endured in the mountains, and he died shortly after returning to San Francisco. In a letter to a Seattle friend, however, he told of finding the gold and included directions and a map.

As word of Jackson's discovery spread, others staked their lives trying to find Slumach's mine. Most failed to return, met with fatal accidents, or died shortly after their journey's end. Each foray was inevitably covered by the press and ignited a new epidemic of gold fever, and although there was no geological evidence to support the presence of a major gold deposit in the Pitt Lake area, since 1891 more than twenty men have lost their lives searching for the lost mine in that vicinity.

In 1947 the *Vancouver Daily Province* magazine section carried an extensive article by Clyde Gilmour entitled "Hoodoo Gold," which not only included an artist's rendition of the Pitt Lake mountain range but also a part of the letter in which Jackson described how he found the gold:

> I climbed to the top of a sharp ridge to get my bearings and found myself looking down into a little valley or canyon I had not seen previously. With some difficulty, I reached the little creek lying in the valley.
>
> Now comes the interesting part. I had only a prospector's small pan, but I found colours immediately. I knew I had struck it rich.
>
> In going up the creek I came to a place where the bedrock was bare. Here I gathered gold by the handful, some pieces as large as walnuts.

Gilmour's article also contained Jackson's directions to the gold:

> You go by boat 40 miles up the Fraser from New Westminster to the outlet of Pitt Lake, then 15 miles the whole length of the lake to the mouth of the Pitt River. Then 18 or 20 miles upstream to the point where the river is no longer navigable.
>
> From there on, you go on foot, over forbidding trails and chasms like those traversed by the novelist James Hilton's travellers in Tibet, on the road to Shangri-La. Slumach's ill-starred mine itself, according to John Jackson's dying directions, is situated somewhere above the 4,000-foot level of a nameless mountain.[18]

Dr. Eric Paetkau recalled, "Herman read where Jackson would have stashed the gold. He looked at the picture and picked out a spot and said, 'That's it! That's where the article said the mine was.'"

In her 1975 *Vancouver Sun* article, Rhody Lake quoted Bergie as saying that the lost gold mine had "gold nuggets as big as walnuts."[19] Her wording mirrored Jackson's description, indicating that either Herman had used those words from Gilmour's article or Bergie had read his "Hoodoo Gold" article herself.

According to Bergie, her father received $16,000 for his Four Mile Point property. With some of the money, Herman purchased a large parcel of undeveloped land that was once part of the Sweetpea Ranch owned by Francis and Alice French. It was located just above the Elvins' summer cottage and near what is now the Sechelt Arena. The Solberg house was towed

Herman's Four Mile Point house was moved across the inlet to the family's Reed Road property. It was moved again to Carlson Creek in 1974, along with Bergie's cabin and a float filled with the Solbergs' collection of junk. Photo courtesy of Bill Walkey.

by barge to a nearby landing and skidded onto the property via Reef Road.

"The Solbergs launched their boats off our dock," said Cavin Crawford. "They used our property like it was theirs and always walked up our driveway to their house."

Once he had settled himself and Olga on the West Porpoise Bay property, Herman set off on his search for the gold mine.

"He and Minnie and Bergie hired a helicopter and had the pilot put them down at the spot where Herman had decided the mine would be," said Dr. Paetkau. "After the helicopter lifted off, they discovered they were bluffed in and couldn't get out. They couldn't move for three days until the helicopter returned to pick them up."

Over the next several years Herman hired various aircraft to return Bergie to the Pitt Lake mountains so she could continue to search for the gold. When the money from the Four Mile Point sale ran out, he tried to find a buyer for his West Porpoise Bay property.

"Herman wanted me to buy thirty acres near the arena," said Dr. Paetkau.

When the doctor refused, Herman listed it for sale with McKnight Realty, but it didn't sell and he finally took it off the market. Six months later he again approached the doctor.

"Okay, Herman," said Dr. Paetkau, "I'll buy the property for the price you had it listed for on the condition that you do not use the money for another trip to Pitt Lake, but use it on a trip to Norway."

The sale went through, and since Dr. Paetkau had only purchased Herman's property as an investment, he allowed the Solbergs to continue living there.

Although Herman eventually honoured the trip to Norway part of his promise, he also coaxed Bergie into taking one more trip to find the gold. In her *Vancouver Sun* article, Rhody Lake again quoted Bergie as she described the journey she had made the previous year:

> It took me two or three days to walk up, clearing the road at the same time. I camped on the mountainside at night and it stormed. Lightning was coming and rocks were rolling down the mountain. I was never so scared. Lightning is the only thing I'm afraid of. The river rose so much I had to pack my dog over, and I fell in, pack sack and all. I left my sleeping bag in a tree. The bears are probably using it for a pillow.[20]

In a 1991 interview Bergie added more details to this story.

> I went up to that mine up in the Pitt Lake area. Tried to find that lost gold mine of Slumach's. Gosh, I went up there—was it in a helicopter or an airplane that time? I can't remember. It was the airplane, I t'ink. Gosh, they set me off there and it was real nice weather. I made a road all the way up to the place I was supposed to go. Then it started pouring rain something terrible. Just dark and a t'under storm and lightning. I never t'ought I was going to get out of that place alive.
>
> My father t'ought for sure he was going to find that Slumach's lost gold mine so he could get rich. See, he didn't want to leave me without any money. But after he spent all that money, he never found anything. I been back there

Aerial view of the west side of Porpoise Bay. From left, top to bottom: Len Van Egmond's small marina; Ted Osborne's small marina in front of his home; a federal government wharf built in 1924, with floats at the end; Tyee Airways float and planes; float for moorage of small craft, which Tyee Airways took over from the federal government; Henry Hall's wharf. Photo courtesy of the *Press* newspaper, the Procter family and Sechelt Community Archives.

> I t'ink two or three times. One time with a helicopter and a couple of times with the airplane, I t'ink. My sister, she doesn't like that because she said my father spent too much money on his gold mine and never found anything. I did find some pretty rocks there, but somebody stole them. I'm sure there must have been something in them. One was a great big rock. Real sparkly.[21]

When Bergie was forty-six, she moved from Sechelt Creek to her parents' home on Reef Road where she was able to help care for Olga. The neighbouring Elvin and Crawford families didn't like the junk Bergie brought with her, but they were grateful for the security she provided, because no intruders dared to come near the property as long as she was close by with her gun.

That year, before his wife became completely incapacitated, Herman decided to honour his agreement with Dr. Paetkau. On June 28, 1969, he, Olga and Bergie boarded a Tyee Airways plane and flew to Vancouver, where they transferred to a commercial jet bound for Oslo.

Shirley Lewis, who worked for Tyee Airways at the time, remembered Bergie's arrival at the Tyee office prior to the flight.

"She was looking pretty bad," said Lewis. "She had lipstick on and up her nose, and although someone had curled her hair with Toni curlers, she had pulled the curlers out, but hadn't combed her hair afterwards. She had a lady's hat on, and an older-style dress that draped over the tummy and over the side, nylons that were not pulled up tight, so they sagged, brogues, a purse, earrings and several necklaces. She was trying to look like a lady."

Lewis and the other office women took Bergie into the washroom and fixed her up.

"We took her makeup off, combed her hair, removed all of the necklaces but one and explained to her that you usually just wore one at a time, then showed her how to put lipstick on."

Bergie said little about the trip to Norway when she returned. She had taken her prospecting clothes in the hope of looking for gold, but there is no indication that she did so.

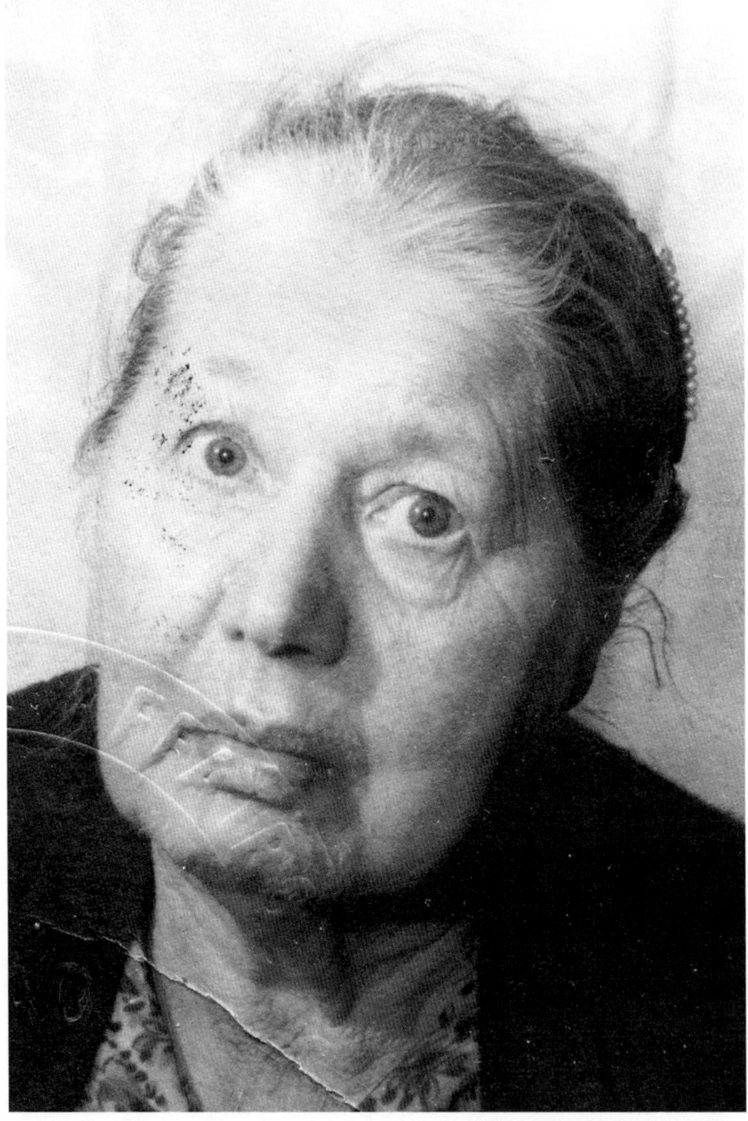

In June 1969, Herman Solberg honoured a promise to take his wife, Olga, back to Norway for a visit. Bergie went along, taking her prospecting clothes with her. Passport photo, December 1968.

Herman Solberg renewed his passport in 1975 and in October 1977 made the last of four trips he took to Norway. He died the following year. Passport photo, October 1975.

Olga's health grew worse after the return from her homeland.

"She had suffered a stroke and could not talk," said Shirley Lewis, who once visited them at the house on Reef Road. "She was in a wheelchair and they'd push her into a corner somewhere when they were busy. I always thought it would be nicer if they'd pushed her over by a window so she could look out."

According to Dr. Paetkau, however, Minnie and Bergie took very good care of their mother.

"They changed her diaper, took her to the toilet—they were always solicitous and very worried. Called me all the time to come and check her blood pressure."

At one point the doctor suggested that the girls would benefit from putting their mother in a nursing home for a few weeks of respite care. "However, whenever they did agree to put her in hospital, they could only stand it for about two days and then they'd take her out. They could not handle her being in there. They didn't trust anyone but themselves to look after her."

Bergie would not have disputed that remark.

"When I took her to the hospital," she said, "if they wanted to know anything it was awfully hard for her to explain anything because she couldn't speak English very good. And she never did like the hospital because they said she was too fat, and they wouldn't give her any cream and no sugar in her tea, so she wouldn't drink it."

Despite the sisters' care, Olga's health continued to fail and she died on December 24, 1970, at the age of seventy-four. She was buried in the Seaview Cemetery in Gibsons.

The following year, Herman used what was left of the money he'd received from the property sale to finance a second trip for himself to Norway, where he stayed with Olga's nephew and niece.

Bergie's home at Carlson Creek had no power or running water. She built an outhouse and makeshift shelters for her animals, using any materials she could get for free. Photo courtesy of Jerry Joyce.

When the Sechelt Arena opened in 1974, the land around it was subjected to closer scrutiny by neighbouring residents. Soon Dr. Paetkau and his partner were being pressured by the village mayor and his council to clean up the mess the Solbergs had created, including a raft filled with Bergie's collection of odds and ends. Two old cars—a Hillman and a Nash Metropolitan—were among her things. Moored next to the Elvins' boathouse, the raft was an eyesore to many waterfront property owners.

"Teddy Osborne once threatened to blow up the float," said Cavin Crawford, "but we said please don't—if you do, she'll move everything onto our place!" Crawford also remembered how upset his mother was when she came to her cottage one winter weekend and discovered Bergie's animal skins spread out in her trees.

Finally Paetkau felt he had no choice and Herman and Bergie were given notice to clean up the mess or vacate the premises. It was only then that Bergie discovered that Herman had sold their home.

Dorothy (Chamberlain) Clode had inherited her parents' property near Carlson Creek, and Bergie turned to her for help.

"Bergie called us in a panic," said Elizabeth Clode, "because her father had sold off his holdings. My mom was extremely kind-hearted and generous and wouldn't have ever turned her down. So Bergie moved onto our property because she had no place else to go."

Moving all of the material Bergie and Herman had collected over the years was not an easy task.

"She started bringing stuff down to a float she had moored between the Porpoise Bay launching ramp and the main dock," said Shirley Lewis. "You should have seen what she put on there—old cars that didn't even run!"

There were no buildings left on the Clode property, and since Dr. Paetkau had no use for the two houses the Solbergs were using on Reed Road, Herman and Bergie decided to move them. The house that Herman had already hauled across the inlet from Four Mile Point was moved first, and in September 1974, Ray Stockwell used his D-8 Cat to winch the second, smaller cabin onto a float. Bergie fired up the *Fjeld*'s Easthope engines and towed the float to Carlson Creek, where the cabin was winched ashore beside her father's house. Then she returned to Porpoise Bay for the float that held their collection of junk.

There was no power at Carlson Creek, and Bergie had to build an outhouse and create makeshift shelters for her animals using any materials that she could get for free. While fishing one summer with his brother, Mike Jackson saw Bergie's boat tied to the cribbing of an abandoned log dump.

"She had found this old trailer up the inlet," he said. "It was just up from Tillicum Bay. I think it had been one of Osborne's old skidder dumps. It was like a big travel trailer, and Osborne had parked it up from the beach about eight or nine feet into the bush."

Curious, Jackson and his brother hiked up the overgrown logging road to where Bergie was winching the trailer out with a come-along. The trailer tires were flat, but Bergie was delighted with her find.

"Oh, sure," she told them happily, "Art said I could have this trailer. If I can get it out of here, I can take it across the inlet and fix it up."

"She was ready to winch it out of the bush and down the hill and onto the log dump and from there onto a raft she had towed over!" marvelled Jackson. "We gave her a hand and got it out onto the dump, but it was quite an effort for the three of us. And here she had been ready to do it herself! When the high water came in, we got it on the float and she tied the float to her speedboat and towed it across the inlet. The float was about twelve feet wide and the trailer was sitting sideways on it, sticking out like airplane wings. Somehow she got it off at her place and winched it up her bank. Several years later I saw she'd fixed it up as a goat shed."

Herman, by this time, was eighty-three years old and his health was beginning to fail. Bergie didn't want to leave him

Mike Jackson found Bergie trying to winch this trailer from the bush and onto a small raft. Once aboard, it stuck out over the side like airplane wings. She used it as a goat shed. Author photo, Carlson Creek, 2005.

alone at Carlson Creek, but he was in no condition to keep up with her when she went to town. In the end she developed a variety of solutions for his care, the most frequent being the use of the office at Tyee Airways.

"Bergie and Herman would come over by boat," said Shirley Lewis. "She'd bring him into our office and sit him in a chair and leave him there while she did shopping. He'd go to sleep most of the time, and we'd check periodically to see that he didn't fall over. I mean, what could you do? She'd just come in, put him on a chair and walk out. She never asked."

As she had with her mother, Bergie did not trust the hospitals or the medical profession to adequately care for her father. Her mistrust increased when he suffered a fracture while in the hospital.

"They broke his leg," she said, "and my father said they were trying to kill him in there. But I didn't know they were that bad they were going to break his leg!"

A letter from John Dafoe, featured in a story about "The Cougar Sisters," tells of a time when he gave Herman a ride home from the hospital and how Mr. Solberg "was enthusiastic about picking up some stout beer for the trip home and he quickly found a bottle of [Dubonnet] Brandy when he arrived home." He also noted that Bergie offered him tea and banana bread.[22]

One night Bergie called Mike Jackson and asked if he'd give her and Herman a lift home from the hospital.

"Herman was making such a ruckus on the wards that the staff threatened to tie him down," said Jackson, "so Bergie calls me late at night and asks if I'd pick her and her dad up. I figured they wanted a lift to the Porpoise Bay wharf, so I agreed. I got to the hospital and we loaded the old man into the jeep."

Herman was in so much pain he was crying, but knowing better than to argue with either Solberg, Jackson started to drive toward the wharf.

"No!" Bergie exclaimed. "Can you give him a lift *home*?"

Jackson stopped the truck.

"Bergie, it's ten o'clock!" he protested, but they were so frantic that he finally agreed. "The road to Chamberlain Bay was a muddy old skid road. We went up the Halfmoon Bay logging road and up No. 9. Every time we hit a bump Herman would be howling in pain. But we got him there and carried the old goat into the cabin and set him down in his favourite chair by their wooden table. Bergie made him some tea and found some animal crackers—they had a real fondness for animal crackers and canned milk and sugar—and we sat there drinking tea and dunking animal crackers. Here was this tough old man, howling like a baby, with his pinkie tucked through the handle of a fancy teacup dunking animal crackers and slurping it down! His hands were so swollen he could hardly get his fingers through the teacup!"

But it wasn't long before Herman was rushed once more to the hospital, only this time his condition was so serious he was transferred to Vancouver. He died at St. Paul's Hospital on April 15, 1978, at the age of eighty-seven.

In the will he had signed on July 27, 1965, Herman left all of his worldly possessions to "my dear daughter Bergliot Solberg." To his "oldest daughter" he left the sum of five dollars. It is possible that he had prepared the will after one of his frequent quarrels with Minnie, but the more likely explanation for leaving his estate to Bergliot was because Minnie was already being cared for by Henry Dray and was therefore no longer Herman's responsibility.

Both daughters deeply mourned his loss, and until the end of their own lives, they blamed the hospital staff and doctors for his death.

A HUNTING LEGEND

Bergie's attitude toward animals was as complex as the rest of her nature. In some instances she was fiercely protective of them, travelling for hours in bitterly cold weather just to secure feed for her goats or to find them new grazing areas. Many of the quarrels she had with people were over what she perceived as their mistreatment of animals she'd either sold or given to them.

"Once she gave away a goat to someone in Gibsons," said her friend Diane Sperring. "When she checked on it, the goat was outside in the rain. So she had me park the truck down the road while she went into the field, got the goat and took it back to her place."

At Sechelt Creek she had spent much of her free time looking after the animals she'd brought with her.

"She had a whole menagerie," said Norm Johnson. "Lots of goats. In every building she left all the doors open so wherever the goats happened to be, that's where they'd stay. Pretty soon the buildings were filthy."

In Rhody Lake's "Woman of the Woods" article, Bergie told of how she once owned a pig.

> I traded one bear skin for a pig. I wish I never did. I cured it myself with alum and saltpetre. But I liked the pig. It used to talk to me every morning till Dad said I had to get rid of it, it was getting so big.
>
> I sure hated to shoot that pig. And wouldn't you think—I didn't shoot him so good? I felt so bad that I just wounded him the first time.
>
> And then the deep-freeze didn't work so I had to can the whole pig. It took me two days.[23]

Billy goats and nannies that no longer produced milk were also butchered and eaten.

Like a cougar, an animal whose main focus is to protect itself from predators and acquire the food it needs to survive, Bergie killed dispassionately, and although she generally tried to do so without causing more pain to the animal than necessary, there were times when even that concern was absent. She had learned from her father that while some animals, such as cougars and mountain goats, deserved respect, others were just nuisances to be exploited or eliminated. Seals were among those she regarded as a nuisance. She saw them as a threat to the fish she was trying to catch, and the fact that the government was willing to pay up to five dollars for the nose of a harbour seal and had done so since 1914[24] confirmed her belief that killing them was of no more consequence than swatting a mosquito.

Bergie sometimes travelled for hours in bitterly cold weather just to secure feed for her goats or to find them new grazing areas. Photo courtesy of Randy Thomas and the *Vancouver Sun*.

West Porpoise Bay resident Eirwen Cleaver with Bergie and her elkhound, Bush, in about 1999. "Bergie told me she was tracking a bear once. She parted some trees and the bear was facing her. She was too near it to point her gun, but she managed to get the barrel up and under the bear's chin, then stepped back and shot it. She said that was the most frightening experience she had." Photo courtesy of Eirwen Cleaver.

One day when Art Asseltine and Ed Laidlaw tied up at her Sechelt Creek dock, Bergie, who had been out in her boat, came up behind them.

"What're you doin', Bergie?" Art asked.

"Seal hunting," she replied, and showed them the seal she had caught. It was still alive.

"Isn't there a bounty on seals?" asked Ed.

"Just the nose," Bergie said, and pulling out her knife, she sliced off the seal's nose and tossed the body back into the inlet.

According to Norm Johnson, Bergie had bearskins on every wall at Sechelt Creek. "They were all turned inside out and you could see she had scraped some of them."

Occasionally, however, a bear's life would be spared—at least for a while—from Bergie's bullets, such as the bear cub Bill Bestwick remembers her acquiring at Sechelt Creek. He recalled, "She had it in this big shed and she'd wrestle around with it. My daughter Karen and any other kids in camp would go over and she'd take them to see her pet bear."

On April 29, 1964, the *Peninsula Times* reported that Bergie had shot a three-hundred-pound bear at Thornhill Creek in Salmon Inlet. "Unaided she rolled him into her rowboat and rowed down the inlet, a distance of about ten miles. Once home, sister Minnie helped haul the bear out of the boat ready to be skinned."[25]

Bergie both respected and feared cougars and her battles with these animals were legendary. Although she hunted them mostly for pelts or to defend her goats, in the *Coastlife* article by Nancy Moote, she said she had eaten cougar meat and while she found it "okay, kind of sweet," she preferred deer meat.[26]

A 1968 *Peninsula Times* article described Bergie's experience with a 150-pound cougar:

> "We were up in the power line area, when suddenly Bush cringed and seemed to lose interest in the hunt ... It isn't like Bush to retreat. He's one of the best dogs I've seen. When he turned from what was sure enough a strong, decaying smell I knew we were on to something."
>
> The smell was coming from a partly devoured and now-rotting deer carcass.

What Bergliot and Bush were on to was a 10-foot cougar.

"It was back of this salal bush. It glared at me from a distance of 15 feet. Then it attacked, its powerful front legs out-stretched."

The hunter, whose trophies include big mountain goat, bear and elk, extended her arms as far as she could high over her head.

"I always wanted to come face to face with a cougar. But not like this."

She shuddered to think what might have happened had she shot and missed the swooping animal. But she did not miss. Her one shot shattered the left side of the feline's face and head.

"I'll have to clean up the big Tom for the Vancouver buyers," she said.

Bergliot, with her kill, equalled the feat her father chalked up some years ago. She said she was glad she had the chance to match her dad's efforts, but she was sure a similar brush with a cougar would come too soon if it ever came again.

Miss Solberg, who lives with her mother and father, said she felt the cougar pelt would bring her $20. She dragged the dead animal from the bush country to the road the morning she shot it, and was given a lift back to where she lives.

… [W]hen the *Times'* photographer asked to take a picture … Bergliot surprised even her father by hoisting the animal up on her shoulders—all 150 pounds of its dead weight—and tossed it on to a nearby car for a picture.[27]

After catching this 150-pound cougar in a bobcat trap, Bergie killed it with a single shot from her .22 rifle, then hauled it through the bush. Photo April 12, 1972, courtesy of the *Peninsula Times*, the Alsgard family and Sechelt Community Archives.

While Bergie was happy to relate the details of her cougar encounter, she did worry about having her age mentioned along with it—a detail that the reporter generously omitted.

In another *Times* article in 1972, Bergie "came upon this 150-pound cougar caught by the paws in her trap. Not anticipating such big game she was armed only with a .22 rifle but one shot from a distance of twenty feet instantly killed the animal. She dragged and packed the cat through the bush unaided but finally obtained assistance to bring it to her home at West Porpoise Bay."[28]

Both Minnie and Bergie were well aware of hunting regulations, Bergie's first conviction having occurred when she was sixteen for the out-of-season killing of a mountain goat on Tzoonie Mountain. They believed, however, that such rules were intended for those who were hunting for sport and should not apply to people such as themselves who were hunting for their livelihood. As a consequence, Bergie's battles with conservation officers were numerous and legendary.

In 1978 conservation officer Jamie Stephen was assigned to the Sunshine Coast, and throughout his eleven-year posting on the coast his relationship with Bergie wavered between friendship and hostility.

"I would say we ended up with an intermittent friendship," he said. "If things were going her way, if I was helping her out, then I was her buddy, her friend. But when the tables were turned, of course, it was a different story."

Bergie was known locally for her accuracy in shooting game and as a youngster Jim Stockwell would go with her to shoot squirrels. She liked to shoot them in the head so the pelt would not be damaged, and she was always vexed with him when he missed and shot them elsewhere.

In a 1974 letter to the editor, Bergie wrote, "I shoot animals in the head so that they don't suffer."

Jamie Stephen was sure she tried to do so, but he didn't believe she always achieved that goal.

"Shooting a deer in the head is difficult if it's moving," he explained. "And that is often not the best place to shoot an

"First time I met her Bergie was trucking down the road with her dog and gun going hunting," said Tuwanek resident Diane Sperring. "In cold weather she would come across in the boat, put her gloves on the wood stove and stand there getting warm. No running lights on her boat. Sometimes she stayed until midnight before heading back home." Photo 1999, courtesy of Diane Sperring.

animal if you want to cleanly kill it. Shooting it in the neck or behind the ear or a little lower down the upper neck is the best. Otherwise, shooting it in the heart, right behind the shoulder blade, is mostly a killing shot to a hunter."

Because Bergie had no telescopic equipment on her firearms she had to shoot at a fairly close range.

"I think quite likely she didn't succeed in killing everything with one shot," said Stephen, but he added that because she used the same firearms all the time, her accuracy with the weapons would have increased.

Once, when Bergie was facing a 150-pound cougar on the beach at Carlson Creek, her gun didn't fire.

"So I put in another shell and the shell got stuck," she told a CBC reporter many years later. "Finally I got a shell in and got him right in the head."[29]

Most of Bergie's guns were inherited from her father and consequently they were her most valued possessions. *Coastlife* reporter Nancy Moote wrote in 1995:

> Solberg's everyday guns, the 30/30 and .22 magnum, lean by the front door. Stored away more securely is the rifle her father brought from Norway. "I think it's called a Krag 6.5," she says. "It's a real nice gun. It's got a bolt action."[30]

"She had an old Winchester Model 94 .30-30," said Stephen. "She had at least one .22, and a 12-gauge shotgun. It's possible that she had a .22 semi-automatic."

In 1979, after Stephen confiscated her .30-30 along with the two bearskins for which she had no licence, Bergie went to Mike Jackson. It was the first time he'd ever seen her cry.

"It wasn't pretty," he said. "It was like a big tough guy crying."

According to the *Peninsula Times,* "Solberg's defense was that she could not see clearly enough in the bush without a magnifying glass to cancel the first tag, and was forced to kill the second bear when it surprised her as she was skinning the first. She then forgot to cancel the first licence upon her return home and forgot to purchase and cancel a licence for the second bear until a week later ...." But Judge Johnson told the court, "She knew what she was doing and she broke the game laws." He noted that Solberg had travelled to Sechelt to obtain the second licence on the same day conservation officer Jamie

Stephen investigated the bearskins because "she knew he was after her." The *Times* article also quotes Judge Johnson as saying, "You'd better get yourself some glasses ... Don't you know that everybody over 50 has to wear glasses?" and reports that "an earlier attempt to charge Solberg with two other bear shootings was dropped when she maintained they were killed last year."[31]

"There was no doubt that she was going to continue to poach," Stephen said, "and that the only way we could have ever stopped her was to lock her up. I remember very keenly discussing my concern about what a custodial sentence might do to someone like Bergie. I think she would have ended her life if she was detained, and I made certain our Crown counsel knew that detention was not an option."

Although it was customary in such cases for the weapons in question to be destroyed, the conservation officer felt that such an action in Bergie's case would be unnecessarily cruel. He stressed the significance of Bergie's rifle as an inheritance from her father. Consequently her conviction was limited to a seventy-five-dollar fine. There was no detention and her father's gun was returned to her. But as Stephen prophesied, it was not the end to her poaching.

For many years, both Bergie and Minnie used Herman's trapping licence to sell their furs, but eventually Minnie acquired her own trapline in the mountains between Salmon and Narrows inlets. In July 1965 Herman signed his trapline over to Bergie.

Most of the time the Solbergs would skin an animal where it was caught, making cuts around the paws and up the inside of the back legs, then peeling the skin off as if it were a shirt. When they returned home, they would "stretch" the skin, keeping the fur on the inside, on a flat board roughly shaped like the animal and tack it in place. Bear and goat skins were stretched by nailing them to a wall. Once the skin was stretched tight, they would scrape off all the flesh and fat, because any lingering fat, especially on otter skins, will cause the skin to burn and render it unmarketable.

For most of her trapping Bergie used old and rusted leghold traps that she had inherited from her father.

"She had quite an assortment," said Jamie Stephen. "In fact, I think she had a couple of very, very old bear traps which were quite rare. She was not a progressive trapper, though on occasion she modified the leghold traps."

Bergie persisted in using the steel-jawed traps even after they had been banned. If the animal she caught was still alive when she checked her trap, she would have to kill it in a way that didn't damage the fur. Occasionally, she would try to save an animal she had caught by mistake.

In May 1982 the conservation officer went to Bergie's home at Carlson Creek to measure the skull of a cougar that she had shot. While he was there, she asked if he knew about a young bear she had accidentally caught in a leghold trap she had set for raccoons. She had taken the cub to the veterinarian in Gibsons and told Stephen that the vet was going to fix it up and find a place for it to live. When Stephen informed her that trapping season for raccoons ended on February 28, Bergie retorted that the raccoons were bothering her chickens.

"I explained to Solberg that she was not permitted to trap beyond the close of the season," wrote Stephen in his subsequent report to Crown counsel, "and because her traps were catching other animals, I forbade her to set them again, saying she would have to shoot the offending predators in the head."[32]

When Stephen decided to check the traps himself, Bergie tried to stall him.

"That traps are away up the road," she said nervously. "At least half a mile. They're sprung anyways."

"Oh, come on, Bergliot," Stephen cajoled, "a short walk would be pleasant on a sunny day."

Despite Bergie's continued protests, they set out. Later he wrote in his report:

> She reluctantly hiked up a logging road about half a mile from her residence to the trap set. At the set I found two leg-hold traps: Trap (a) was a double spring model having teeth on both jaws and a chain of 130 cm., while Trap (b) was a single spring (less powerful) model having teeth on both jaws and a chain length of 150 cm. Both traps were rusted so that the manufacturer's name was not clear but it seemed to me they would have been either Victor or Newhouse traps of about #3 ½ size—a trap overly powerful for catching and holding raccoons. Solberg had told us on the way up the logging road that she had set them so far away because she hoped to catch the raccoon that had dragged another leg-hold trap away that she had earlier set. She stated she felt they often frequented this area of the bush. Both traps were in a closed position, since Solberg had not re-set them after having removed the wounded bear cub; both traps had their chains attached to a long tangled piece of heavy galvanized wire which in turn was attached to a tree trunk.

> I asked Solberg why she had set traps she knew to be illegal, and she told me she didn't want me to take her traps away. I pointed out they had teeth on the jaws and she stated she didn't know they both had teeth, remembering only that the one she had caught the cub in (the one that she had recently had welded) had teeth, but not the other one. I showed her both and she mumbled that she had forgotten about the teeth. We talked about the chain lengths and I told her how the animals could run after being caught and if there was a long chain, they would invariably jerk their limb out of its socket once they came to the end of the chain. I asked Solberg which trap it was that caught the cub and held up the double spring trap and she told me that was the one.
>
> Bait which had been used in the trap set consisted of a dead chicken, deer skin pieces, and a dead grebe—a migratory bird for which there is no hunting season. I asked Solberg about the grebe and she at first denied knowing it was even there, later defending its use as bait by saying they were no good for anything, all they did was eat the little fish in the creek. I had told Solberg on earlier occasions that she was to discontinue her practice of shooting sea birds which she called "fish ducks," in her misguided efforts to protect salmonid fry from normal predation.[33]

Bergie became visibly upset when the conservation officer decided to confiscate her traps.

"Oh, don't take these away from me!" she pleaded. "I've had these for so long. They're some of the best I've got."

Stephen refused to relent, and Bergie shouted, "Well, I guess I should've just let the little bear go then and never said nothing about it to anyone and let it die in the bush somewhere."

Later that afternoon Stephen contacted Gibsons veterinarian Dr. Dennis Bailey, who said he'd put the cub to sleep because one of its front paws was dead from having the blood supply cut off.

Stephen's report continued:

> I picked up the cub approximately a week later, and estimate it to weigh about 7 lbs.—it having been born sometime toward the end of February.
>
> Although the traps used are illegal for trapping, I am aware that Solberg is extremely upset at their seizure, since they were passed on to her by her deceased father; and I would therefore recommend that they be returned to her provided they are not used for trapping again. Had the traps not had teeth, there is a greater probability that the young cub might have survived its excruciatingly painful ordeal, although there is little doubt that it would still have been permanently maimed. Solberg knows the regulations concerning teeth on the jaws and chain lengths—these two regulations are contained in the Trapping Regulations Synopsis … which is mailed out to each trapper each year. Solberg also knows that she was trapping during the closed season, but it appears she was more interested in retrieving a leg-hold trap dragged away by an earlier animal victim than she was in catching incidental wildlife at a remote location from her chicken coop. I do not recommend that she

LEGHOLD TRAPS

Leghold traps are comprised of two metal jaws held apart by a small central plate that is connected to a spring and baited, usually with some type of meat. The weight of an animal stepping on the plate releases the spring, causing the jaws to snap shut on the victim's leg, foot or any other body part that happens to be in the way. If it is not killed outright, which is often the case, the animal will suffer great pain and frantically try to release itself, sometimes chewing or twisting off its own limb to break free, only to die later from blood loss, gangrene, starvation or predation by another animal.

In 1982 the use of traditional steel-jawed leghold traps was prohibited and a modified form was restricted to special situations, such as trapping otters where the trap is placed near the water and attached to a special chain. The trapped animal instinctively runs into the water and though it is able to drag the chain underwater, when it tries to resurface for air, the chain acts as an anchor, and the animal drowns.

Conservation Officer Jamie Stephen described the modified traps in a 2003 interview: "Essentially, those jaws are padded with rubber and are offset so they don't close diametrically opposite to each other. They literally hold the animal securely but don't cut into flesh, and they don't break leg bones the way they used to."

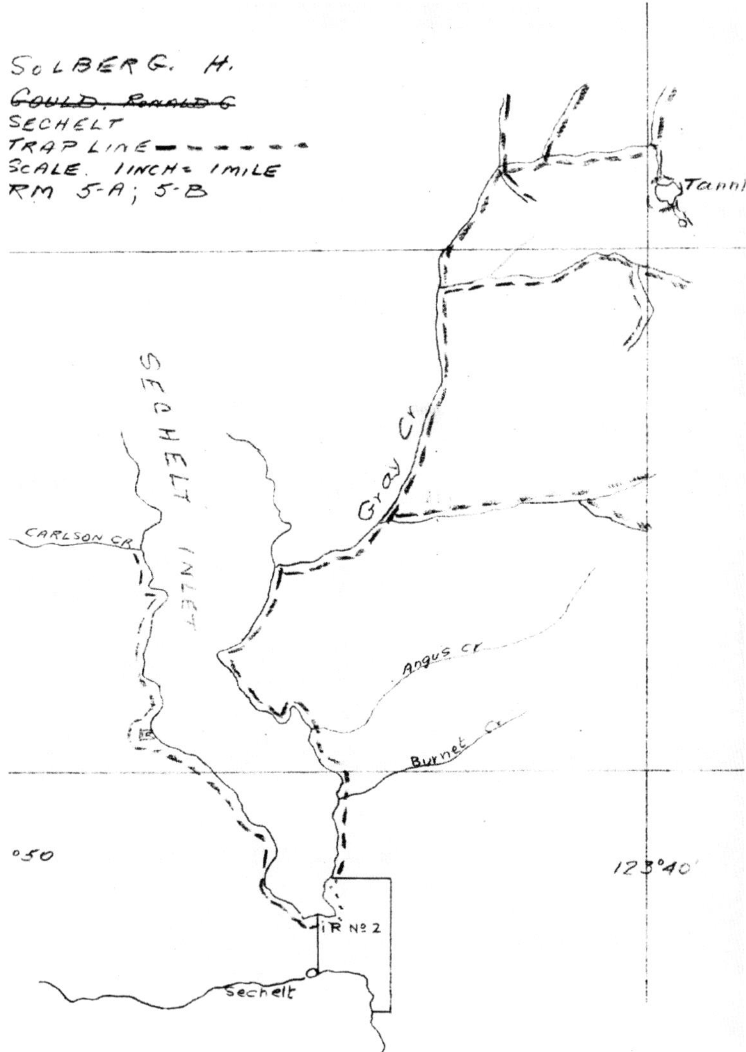

Herman Solberg's trapline, acquired in 1935, was transferred to Bergie in 1965. By 1983 the foreshore boundaries on both sides of Porpoise Bay were excluded because of foreshore leases and upland development. Map courtesy of BC Ministry of Water, Land and Air Protection.

> be prohibited from trapping—hunting and trapping are her life and although she has a history of wildlife violations behind her, she is coming around to a degree of compliance with Wildlife and Fisheries Act regulations. I would recommend a fine which would deter her from committing other such violations again."[34]

Once again Stephen's intervention saved Bergie from losing her licence and her equipment. Her punishment was a five-hundred-dollar fine and fifty hours of community work for the Fish and Wildlife branch for the province of BC. Although she paid the fine, a Probation Report to Crown counsel dated February 28, 1983, indicated that the "Subject has refused to do Community Work as ordered."

It wasn't only the conservation officers who were disturbed by Bergie's treatment of wild animals. One day Keith Thirkell asked Bergie what she charged for a bobcat pelt and she replied, "Seventy-five dollars."

"I'll pay you one hundred and fifty," Thirkell told her.

Several weeks later Bergie called and asked, "Do you still want that bobcat?"

"Yes," he said, "but I'm really busy today. Can I come tomorrow?"

"Oh, gosh," she responded, "he's in a trap, but maybe he'll last."

Appalled, Thirkell shouted, "For God's sake, Bergie! Shoot him and put him out of his misery!"

On another occasion when Thirkell was photographing Bergie with her long rifle, Bergie put the gun to her shoulder and asked, "Do you want me to shoot that seagull?" Before he could respond she had blasted a seagull off of a nearby piling.

There were times when Bergie succeeded in eluding the conservation officer. The late Richard (Dick) Hammond, who used to fish and hunt in the same territory where Bergie and Minnie hunted, remembered a story she told about hunting a mountain goat near the Tzoonie River. Bergie had shot a goat and was ready to haul it down the mountain to her boat when she saw the conservation officer arrive in his own boat. She decided to wait him out, and when he came up the river looking for her, she hid.

"Going up that stream is steep, dangerous and slippery," said Hammond, "and the game warden wasn't having any of it. Instead, he camped for two days at the bottom. Bergie ate raw goat meat rather than light a fire and let him know where she was. But she waited him out. When she saw him heading back down the inlet, she came down with her goat."

Occasionally Bergie went hunting with a partner. Richard Elvin was twelve when he purchased a new .22 automatic.

"Bergie thought it was a neat rifle and she taught me to shoot it," he said. "Then we went hunting. She always got excited when she was hunting, especially if she was on the trail of something. She'd jump from log to log with no trouble. I'd try to follow and fall flat on my face, and she'd laugh."

If her hunting partner had a vehicle that could be used to transport her kill, Bergie was even more amenable to their company. Mike Jackson was only fourteen when he went with her for the first time.

"I liked to go hunting with my dad," he said, "but he was always hard pressed for time to go out with me. One day he jokingly told me to go with Bergie. So the next morning I

Hoping to build a cabin on Piper Point, Bergie exchanged her Gray Creek trapline for one extending northward from Snake Bay. When the change was made she discovered regulations forbade fulltime occupation of trappers' cabins. Author photo.

got up and made some coffee, took my .30-30 and went over there. I shouldn't have been driving, but I did. We went up the mountain and I got my first deer. She had her little dog, Bush, with her on a leash, and she was going up over this rock bluff when I shot the deer. She was down on that deer and had it gutted out and on the logging road before I could even catch up to her."

According to Jackson, "Hunting with Bergie was like tagging along behind a human bear. She'd plow through the bush dragging the dog with her, and climb up rock bluffs, and that little dog'd be hanging there from his leash! She'd never think anything about walking four or five miles into the bush, get something and then drag it back. She'd keep going right until dark and never worry about how she was getting back."

One day in late October when Bergie was working as a whistlepunk for Gus Crucil, she and the crew were coming down from Gray Creek when a large black bear crossed the road in front of the crummy.

"Bergie just about jumped out on top of it," said Rudy Crucil.

The next day Crucil's crew was moving the spar tree, and since Bergie wasn't needed, she brought her gun and her dog and had the driver drop her off near the spot where they'd seen the bear. Her plan was to track the bear and return at four o'clock to catch a ride back down the mountain with the crummy. It was raining and cold that day, and when she didn't appear at the appointed time, the crew decided she had walked out and gone home. The next morning they saw her walking down the road. She had spent the night on the mountain with her dog and the bear she'd shot.

"She and Minnie used to do that quite often," said Rudy. "She couldn't get this one out of the woods by herself, so she walked home and got Minnie to give her a hand. I'm not sure which way they took it out."

One evening in the late 1960s, Dr. Paetkau had made a house call to check on Olga at the Solbergs' home on Reed Road.

"Minnie was at home," he said, "but Bergie had taken her little putt-putt with an Easthope engine and gone hunting up Narrows Inlet to get a goat. The mountains there are about five thousand feet, and she went quite high up. She got her goat and cleaned it and started down the mountain, but soon her dog, Nori—a Norwegian elkhound—packed it in and couldn't go another step. So she hoisted him up along with the goat and her rifle and her pack and carried them down to her boat. It was raining and dark when she came around Storm Bay and her engine conked out. She set up a tarp over the motor, took the carburetor apart and fixed it, then continued on her way. It was just after ten o'clock when she came into the cabin carrying the dog, the goat and her rifle!"

Bergie followed her father's tradition in always calling her dogs "Bush." If she had two, one would be "Bush" and the other would receive a different name. Returning home after dark or in the fog she would use them to navigate her route. From her boat she would call out and the dog (or dogs) would bark in response from the shore. She could then determine where she was by the timbre of the bark and make her way safely to the dock.

Occasionally, Jamie Stephen encountered Bergie in remote areas when it was pitch black.

"She would be coming down a mountain when I was waiting for the last vehicular hunters coming out of the bush," he said. "Bergliot would come around the corner, and we'd often chat. More often than not she had one or two dogs with her, and she always had a firearm."

Cavin Crawford remembered that Bergie often came home long after dark.

"At low tide the front of our place had about a quarter-mile of mud," he said. "Sometimes, around midnight, you'd hear Bergie's putt-putt boat. The engine would stop and you'd hear her cursing because she missed the mooring, and then a 'whoosh whoosh' and you knew she was rowing. After she landed she'd pack a deer or bear up our driveway to her place with no flashlight or anything!"

Like Bergie, Minnie also endured severe conditions while hunting. Tor Skei remembered a time in the 1980s when she arrived at his family's salmon farm on the west side of Sechelt Inlet at Big Bear Bay. The temperature was -3°C, and she had travelled down from Jervis Inlet in an open boat.

"We almost had to physically lift her out, she was so frozen," he said.

They gave her some hot soup to warm her, and when she'd eaten, Minnie told them that she'd been in her backyard when a cougar came into the garden. Her dog had chased the cougar up a tree and Minnie went into the house, got her gun and came outside and shot it.

"But it was so dark," she complained, "that when it fell from the tree it just about hit me!"

When Tor and his father helped her back into the boat, she showed them the skin, head and all.

"She was taking it in to get it tanned."

While many of Bergie's animal skins were sold to the Vancouver Fur Exchange, to an Edmonton fur exchange or to the Hudson's Bay Company, many others were sold to individuals within the community. Some people, such as Oddvin Vedo, who was the economic development commissioner for the Sunshine Coast Regional District (SCRD) in the early 1980s, would send customers her way, but it was also not uncommon for her to appear in one of the local business offices and remark that she'd just shot a bear or a cougar or a goat. Eventually this would lead to someone approaching her to purchase the skin.

"A bobcat pelt on my wall was one of Bergie's," said Dean Robilliard. "She trapped that and I bought the pelt off her and had it mounted."

"Sometimes she'd sell her bear hides to local people to make into rugs," said Bergie's former neighbour, Sheila Page. "Only they weren't really cured. Maybe dried, but not treated."

Bergie often shared her wild game with friends, especially Dorothy Chamberlain Clode.

"When she was younger she'd send up haunches of venison on the bus," said Elizabeth Clode. "We'd get a call from Pacific Stage Coach Lines that we had a package and we'd go down to the depot and pick it up. By then it would be dripping, but we always had nice venison for Christmas—whether it was legal or not."

Elizabeth Clode also remembered that when she was a child Bergie would tell her stories of her adventures with animals. "Once she told us about killing a bear with a hand axe. Bergie had been fishing a salmon spawning stream on the property and was pulling her boat up on the beach when a bear came up behind her. All she had with her was a hand axe. Of course, if the bear thought she had any fish, it would be in attack mode, so she wasn't taking any chances. She swung around and beaned it with the hand axe and killed it. She was quite proud of that."

As an adult, there were times when Bergie used her bounty to play jokes on her neighbours, especially when she was living on Reed Road. "She had quite a high stockade fence at that place," said Jamie Stephen, "and she used to don a bearskin and pretend she was a bear behind the fence or in the bush to scare passersby."

One day, however, Stephen played a joke of his own on Bergie.

Dorothy Clode and Jerry Joyce. After Dorothy's death, the Clode family sent property manager Jerry Joyce to check on Bergie. They bought her an outboard motor, put a new roof on her cabin and installed a new float. Photo 1990, courtesy of Jerry Joyce.

"I knew that Bergliot had some interest in royalty," he said, "because once when we were at her place she showed my wife, Helen, a pretty valuable coronation cup that had been passed down from her dad."

Sometime later Helen's uncle came to visit them from England.

"Eric was a Londoner with an aristocratic bearing," Stephen explained. "He was about sixty-four at the time and always wore a blazer and tie and slacks. He had never been to Canada, never seen any of the Canadian wilds, and I thought I'd give this fellow a bit of an adventure. So I took him out on patrol with me. It was in the middle of the hunting season and, in due course, right out in the wilderness, we came across Bergliot. As a hoax, I introduced Eric as the president of the World

Wildlife Federation from London, England. I said he'd heard about Bergliot's poaching adventures and he'd come over to talk to her on behalf of Her Majesty the Queen. Bergliot was absolutely struck dumb. She didn't know how to respond. She was very deferential and Eric played the role expertly."

Stephen never told Bergie about his joke, but any hope he had that Her Majesty's interest might reform the old poacher were soon dashed. Before the season was out he was once again writing up an incident report after Bergie appeared in town to purchase cougar tags to go hunting for cougar, coincidentally on the same day that she sold two cougar pelts to a couple of local residents.

NOTORIETY

Bergie and Minnie attracted a lot of attention, partly because they wore dresses that were at least two decades out of style or work pants, heavy sweaters and battered felt cowboy hats, and partly because of their unusual lifestyle. It was well known that they could hunt, fish, trap and log as well as any man, and their escapades were often worthy of mention in newspapers both on and off the Sunshine Coast. When the articles showed them in a favourable light, the Solbergs were generally happy—that is, until the day they discovered that the writers were earning money for stories about them.

Shortly after Dr. Paetkau moved to the coast in 1959, a local resident and *Winnipeg Free Press* columnist, Ed Green, told him of an article he'd written about Bergie and Minnie.

"He told me they didn't mind him writing the story," said Paetkau, "but they were very annoyed when they found out he got paid for the article and they got none of the money. They wouldn't talk to him anymore after that."

Bergie liked her notoriety, but she wasn't happy when she discovered that writers were being paid for stories that she told for free. Photo courtesy of Bill Walkey.

Because she lived closer to town, Bergie seemed to get the most attention from the press, and her skill as a hunter was a favourite topic. In 1952 *Coast News* columnist Alice French, writing under the penname "Aries," reported:

> The cougar which has been around the inlet [preying] on small dogs and other animals has been killed by Barnalotte Solberg. We always have difficulty spelling this girl's name, but most of us [hereabouts] know her as Myrtle. There are two of the [Solberg] girls, and both of them are wonderful shots. They have for many years kept down marauding coons and other depredatory animals. We hope Myrtle gets a suitable reward; it's a quite a feat for a small girl.[35]

The *Peninsula Times,* on August 4, 1971, provided a brief report of Herman Solberg's second trip to Norway in forty years, and a few years later included a picture of Herman and a friend who was visiting from his home country.

At times the papers carried stories of Bergie's trapping dilemmas. On November 7, 1973, they reported:

> Bergliot Solberg, Sechelt's distaff trapper, hasn't been doing so well lately. Last year she caught one otter and a few mink. "I can't make a living that way," she says. Kids steal her traps and take the animals. A former whistlepunk in a logging camp, Bergliot says she would like to return to a logging camp. Her trapline runs all the way around Porpoise Bay from Sechelt to Piper Point five miles and on the other side of Gray Creek. She shoots seals with a .22, "but nobody wants to buy them anymore."[36]

For several weeks the paper carried stories of Bergie's hunting exploits, which eventually generated a critical letter to the editor denouncing Bergie for trapping. With the help of a friend, Bergie responded with a letter of her own:

> Sir: This is in reply to Jacquelyn McLeod Stephens (The *Peninsula Times,* January 2) who said she was glad I find trapping unprofitable.
>
> I never said I was going to quit hunting and trapping. The only time I trap is in the winter time. I only hunt for meat and I trap for their fur. I am not like these kids that steal my traps and put them up

again on trails or other places where people walk. They don't throw the traps in the water, they use the traps to trap in the summer. It is against the law to trap in the summer and destroy all the animals. That is when they get their young ones. If you know the law, it is also against the law to steal traps on my trap line. I don't put my traps where the hikers go.

I did not mean to shoot that bear in the foot. I did not know my gun was shooting low. I've got another gun now and it shoots good. I shoot animals in the head so that they don't suffer.

How about the cougars on Vancouver Island? A cougar bit a little kid and the kid had to be taken to the hospital.

I came on a place where the cougar had killed a deer. Then the cougar came leaping right for me so I shot him. I was only about 15 feet away when I shot him in the head, so you can see how dangerous it is to walk in the woods without a gun.

Cougars are supposed to kill 36 deer in one year. When cougars kill deer they sometimes rip them in two and some will bite the deer in the head and suck the blood out through the head. I have heard some deer holler for about 15 to 20 minutes. I went the next day and found the carcass with the deer and cougar tracks all around.

I am not the only one that is trapping and hunting. It seems like in your letter that I am.

Bergliot Solberg, Sechelt.[37]

Timber Days were once an annual event in Sechelt, and Bergie was a frequent competitor in loggers' sports events. According to the *Coast News* reporter, she would have won this hand-falling competition if her cut had been lower. Photo May 31, 1977, courtesy of the *Coast News*.

Rhody Lake, in her *Vancouver Sun* article "Woman of the Woods," described Bergie as "a strong woman in her middle years who has the look of the woods and logging camps about her and a hunting knife on her hip. When she walks, she advances vigorously, thrusting the upper part of her body forward, from years of backpacking in the woods."[38]

In the late 1970s pictures of Bergie often appeared in the local press along with mention of her skills as a competitor in the Sechelt Timber Days axe-throwing, nail-driving and falling contests. A frequent winner in the ladies' events, in 1976 she earned the title Lady Logger of the Day.

Bergie was always looking for more storage sheds and in 1977 she decided to collect one of the abandoned buildings from the old Universal Timber logging camp. There she discovered a log raft and, believing that it had also been abandoned, winched the building onto it. Just as she finished the job, a logger from Clowhom showed up and claimed ownership of the float. Ignoring his demands that she remove the house and leave the float where it was, she towed it home. That August the house was destroyed by fire and the papers reported that the cause of the blaze was under investigation. Although no charges were ever laid, Bergie was sure she knew who had set the fire.

Not all of Bergie's escapades were reported in the press, but they did become stories that were passed around the community with great amusement. One of Mike Jackson's favourite tales was about the time he tried to teach her how to drive on his family's dryland sort at Gray Creek, where Bergie was working as a camp watchperson:

She always wanted to drive. It was one of the big things with her. She'd buy an old beater and say she wanted to drive the car to get her goat feed. One day she bought this old Volkswagen bug, a 1950-or-something, and had it towed to [Gray] Creek, and she asked me to teach her to drive. So we got in the car and I gave her the low down: here's the brake, here's the clutch, here's the throttle and shift lever and steering wheel. What you need to do is push the clutch in, put it in gear, then let the clutch out slowly, give it some gas and go.

"Oh, sure, that shouldn't be too hard," she said.

So she slid behind wheel and got it in first gear and away she went. But instead of hitting the brake she hit the throttle! She went roaring around the dry land sort, and that old bug was revving at about seven thousand rpms. The faster she went, the harder she put [the] throttle down, thinking it was the brake. She roared up the logging road and went about five hundred feet uphill before she stalled it. When I caught up to her, she was gripping the steering wheel, her knuckles just white.

I said, "Bergie, don't use throttle, use the brake."

"I don't know what to do!" she said.

"You gotta brake," I repeated. "Put it in reverse, take your foot off the brake and let the clutch out."

So she started going downhill backward at about thirty miles per hour. At the bottom of the hill was a brow log, and on the other side of the brow log was the drop to the beach. We came down that hill like Laurel and Hardy and boom! We hit the brow log! The Volkswagen was high-centred and it was just screaming, the tires revolving.

Bergie got out and said, "That's all the driving I want to do!"

That Volkswagen sat there for a long time before she had it taken to Chamberlain Bay.

After a regular ferry service to the Sunshine Coast was established in 1949, the population of Sechelt began to increase. The settlement became an incorporated village municipality in 1956, and almost at once rules and regulations that had previously been ignored were enforced. A number of the legends about Bergie and Minnie had to do with the way in which they adapted—or failed to adapt—to these changes.

"Like the time the police intercepted her rifle," said Jim Wilkinson. "She had quite a fight over that. She used to walk down the street in Sechelt carrying her rifle. She didn't know that the laws had changed and that it was now illegal to carry a rifle on the street. So one day some green police officer saw her and immediately apprehended her and took her rifle away. Well, to take a rifle away from Bergie was pretty nasty work."

Within a few days Bergie's rifle was returned to her, along with a warning that she had to leave it at home, but the legends that were spun from the incident lasted much longer.

On November 9, 1966, the *Peninsula Times* reported that Bergliot Solberg had been brought before the court on a charge of assault.

> ... [A]ccompanied by her husband, [Mrs. Eva May Owre] was accosted by Miss Solberg who blocked her way while walking into Sechelt. Not only was she called filthy names, but was struck a number of blows on the

arm as she attempted to force her way past Solberg. Her husband finally attempted to go to her aid, but was threatened by the rifle held by the accused.

Corporal Keith Deevey of the Sechelt RCMP Detachment stated in evidence he had spoken to Mr. and Mrs. Owre and had been shown Mrs. Owre's arm, which was badly bruised both above and below her elbow.

Mr. Owre supported his wife's statement, adding that as he moved toward Solberg she pointed her rifle at him and [threatened], "Touch me and I'll plug you."

This was denied later by Miss Solberg who alleged she had been struck first by Mrs. Owre as she pushed passed her on the lane. Trouble arose some years ago when she alleged Owre had struck one of her young goats, causing its head to bleed badly. "He also teases our dogs with sticks," she added.

She agreed she had accused the [Owres] of being cruel and mean as they passed her but had not used bad language or threatened with the gun.

Magistrate Mittelsteadt ruled he considered Solberg to be guilty as charged but that it appeared there was fault on both sides. He therefore put her on a six month suspended sentence on her own [recognizance] of $100. Both parties were ordered to refrain from contact with each other in future if they are unable to get along.[39]

Many stories about Bergie and her animals were humorous, such as the time she asked a chiropractor to give one of her goats a treatment because its back was injured, but others were profoundly sad. One day she and her elkhound Bootsie

At her Carlson Creek home, Bergie kept a sharp eye out for cougars and bears and for boats travelling up or down Sechelt Inlet. Photo courtesy of Randy Thomas and the *Vancouver Sun*.

were at the Jackson Brothers dryland sort where she was working as a watchperson. The loader operator was breaking down a pile of logs when one of the logs fell off the loader and landed on the dog.

"She was upset for months about it," said Mike Jackson. "She figured the machine operator did it on purpose and she had it in for him for years."

Jim Wilkinson was present when another of her dogs died.

"She called me and said Bush wouldn't get up. He just lay there, she said, and he had a lump on his stomach. Bergie wanted the vet to come out to Carlson Creek, but he refused. Somehow she managed to get that dog down to the boat and into town. She had to leave Bush with the vet, who said the dog was in the final days of cancer. That night Bush died. The next day I went down to the wharf to meet Bergie and tell her the news. She sat in my car and cried and cried. I'd never seen her cry before. But she sure had a hard time of it, getting over Bush. She was certain that the vet had killed him."

Over the years, Bergie's story was featured in magazines as far away as Norway and France and she appeared on several Canadian radio and television newscasts.

In 1986 CBC television reporter Jerry McIntosh interviewed her for an episode of *The Best Years*.

As they checked out her otter traps, Bergie told the reporter that she would not like to live in the city because she could not keep any animals there. "I like my trapline and I like to go hunting."

Bergie said that due to the disappearance of otters, she could no longer survive by hunting and trapping as she had when she was younger, and had to go on social assistance. She blamed the fish farms for eliminating the otters. In that year there were thirty-two salmon farms operating on the Sunshine Coast, many of them located in the waters of Salmon, Narrows and Sechelt inlets.

Bergie also told the reporter that the reason she had never married was because the men she took a special liking to never hung around.

The show, which aired on January 29, 1986, ends with Bergie listening to a recording of herself singing a Wilf Carter song.[40]

The following Christmas Eve, Oddvin Vedo took CBC television producer Cam Cathcart and a photographer/sound man to Carlson Creek to interview Bergie.

On his blog Vedo describes walking around with the producer.

"On the beach I counted 28 whole or parts of boats, canoes and other floating devices … all wrecked.

"The cabin was smaller than it looked—a screened bedroom, a kitchen nook, and the entry and main area between a front and back door … the wind could blow right through … One of the dogs … grabbed the captain's chair at the table and sat there, head high. Around the walls were nails or spikes into the woodwork, serving as hangers, some work clothing, and all kinds of collector's items … there were calendars, postcards, eagle feathers, some telephone numbers, rubber bands …"[41]

Vedo was so touched when Bergie revealed that she had never received a Christmas present that he made a return visit with a gift of Norwegian fish balls. She was delighted.

Bergie was also the closing act for a 1988 episode of the CBC's *On The Road Again* series hosted by Wayne Rostad. In the segment,

Bergie told CBC's *On the Road Again* host Wayne Rostad that she was never lonely because there were always too many things for her to do. "You get up in the morning and the day doesn't last too long." Photo courtesy of Bill Walkey.

she played the guitar, sang and yodelled "The Beautiful Yoho Valley" and declared that she was never lonely because there were always too many things for her to do.

"You get up in the morning and the day doesn't last too long," she said.

Rostad pointed out several items in her collection of scavenged merchandise, including two Vauxhalls, a Triumph motorcycle, two Volkswagon Beetles, twelve boats, three washing machines and a television set, all of which Bergie thought she might use one day. Her collection of animals was also shown, consisting at that time of two dogs (Bush and Rocky), eight goats, twelve rabbits and eleven chickens. He ended the segment with a song he'd written and composed about the Cougar Lady:

> She's rosy-cheeked and sixty-four
> Living on the Sunshine Coast
> In a ramshackle cabin by the sea
> With her dogs and goats and chickens,
> And her beachcomber pickings,
> Life is in perfect harmony.
> She's a source of inspiration
> To every man and every woman
> And she lives in contradiction
> To the manners of the land.
> She's a pioneering spirit,
> She's a total independent,
> And if anyone can blaze a trail
> The Cougar Lady can.
> Nobody can blaze a trail
> Like the Cougar Lady can.[42]

In her 1995 *Coastlife* article, reporter Nancy Moote also described Bergie's house.

> Her cabin is jammed with the detritus of a lifetime, leaving just enough room for Solberg to move from her front door to the stove to her bed … [Her] only heat comes from the thin blue flame of her propane cook stove, and she complains that Carlson Creek is a terrible place in the winter when the southeasters blow.

> She hauls water from the creek in buckets for herself, the dogs, the chickens, the rabbits and her seven goats.[43]

Wendell Welander remembered when the producers of the CBC television series *The Beachcombers* approached him for the use of two Beaver aircraft for their show. One plane had already been named *Blossom*, and they asked Welander to give the other one a name as well.

"So I asked my staff to each throw a name in a hat and we'd choose one," he said, but before all of the names were in the hat, he was struck by a better idea. "Forget about the hat, guys! What do you think of *Bergie* for a name? The Beaver is a tough old bush girl, and there's no tougher old girl than Bergie!"

There was a unanimous cry of approval from the staff.

Although Coast Western Airlines is no longer operating, the plane—still bearing Bergie's name—is now owned by Welander's company, Nozama Ventures, and flies out of Yellowknife.

In his 1992 *Coast News Weekender* column, "Voices Up the Inlet," the late Carl Christmas wrote a humorous account of a CB exchange in which Bergie was discussing the use of an elastic band to neuter a goat. A few nights later Bergie appeared at his doorstep to complain about the inaccuracies in the article. In his next column, published on October 1, 1992, Christmas corrected his errors:

> She was very disturbed at having been made to seem like a fool by my description of her painless attempt to neuter her billy goat. The conversation overheard by

Wendall Welander was asked to name his de Havilland Beaver CF MPD, which was being used in the CBC's *Beachcombers* series. His staff at Coast Western Airlines unanimously approved his choice to call it *Bergie*. Ironically, the plane was once owned by the RCMP. Photo courtesy of Roland Lussier.

other CBers in the inlet and Tranquility Base, as well as myself, had been taken out of context.

Her only problem with the neutering was the fact she has used too light a rubberband. It was fine for holding a head of lettuce together, but not to do the job at hand.

It was close to eleven, wrote Christmas, when she left his home.

Fortunately the inlet was like a mill pond. She still had a couple of miles to go, but the stars were bright, the tide was rising, and she'd make it to her float near her farm house.

> Her five goats were still to be fed, a nanny to milk, and eggs to be gathered. How many 69-year-old ladies would you find doing that these days?[44]

According to Christmas, Bergie's two fears in life were encountering cougars after dark along the trail between her house and barn, and having inaccurate information about her printed in the paper.

Photographer Keith Thirkell also earned Bergie's wrath with his article "The Sisters Time Forgot," published in the June 11, 1995, edition of the *Province*. In his description of the Solberg sisters he wrote, "Their faces are wrinkled road maps of history with features as rugged as the coast itself."

Thirkell thought it was a compliment to them, but Bergie and Minnie didn't agree.

"Bergie wanted to kill me for that," he said. "She demanded that the editor print a retraction. Which, of course, he did not do."

As Bergie's fame grew, so did the number of requests for interviews and photographs with her.

"I used to watch tourists come in and see her and want to have their picture taken with her," said Frieda Fawkes, who runs the lottery centre at Trail Bay Mall in Sechelt.

According to George Page, who often played the part of Santa Claus for the Trail Bay Mall during the Christmas season, even the local merchants occasionally contributed to the Solberg legend.

"The storekeepers used to take great delight in telling Bergie that Santa wanted her to sit on his knee," he said. "So she did, and they thought it was a great joke on me. She sat and giggled until she had her picture taken and then she was gone."

In 1978, Bill Walkey arrived at Carlson Creek with a large bag of cream cakes. "Bergie couldn't believe they were all for her," he said. "She gobbled them up." His reward was permission to take all the photographs he wanted that day.

"She had lovely blue eyes," he remembered, adding that she had few social graces and was very frank. "When I brought my cousin, who has a severe spinal curvature, to see her, she jabbed a finger at his back and demanded to know what was wrong with him."

Brian Lee wrote in the *Harbour Spiel Online*, "Even a seven-year-old kid could tell she was the real deal. At an age when fantasies of cowboys and traplines reigned as the ideal lifestyle pursuit, Bergie and Minnie were Daniel Boone and Davy Crockett. And they were women. As we'd drive by, some sibling would point and squeal, 'The Cougar Lady!'"[45]

Bergie was not above going to the press when it suited her purpose, especially when that purpose was to find her goats. Occasionally she even paid for an advertisement, such as this one published in the *Coast News* on February 10, 1981:

> There is a reward for anyone that knows the whereabouts of the Alpine Goat named Matilda and her little nanny kid Cheki, that I loaned out to David Richardson for milk. She is brownish and white. Bergliot Solberg.

At other times she persuaded local reporters to do a story about her troubles. In 1998 Anna Diehl wrote an article entitled "Gotta get their goats," published in the *Reporter*.[46] In that case Bergie had given two pygmy goats to someone as pets and wanted to find out if they were receiving proper care. And a few years later when Bergie was searching for a home for Minnie, writer Jan DeGrass published "'Cougar ladies' on the prowl for new Sechelt home" in the *Coast Independent*.[47]

In October 1996, Bergie participated in a "makeover" event as part of the "Women in the Marketplace" trade and fashion show coordinated by hairdresser Wendy Young. Almost from their first meeting, when she accepted a ride in Wendy's new convertible, Bergie had bombarded the hairdresser with questions about makeup. "She wanted to know how I got that paint on my fingernails without getting it on my skin … what this cream was for, how you use that powder." One day Wendy was in the Lighthouse Pub with her new employee, Patti Lunan, and Patti's mother, who in fun bet two dollars that her daughter wouldn't have the nerve to ask Bergie to be a model for the makeover event. Patti asked and to everyone's surprise, Bergie accepted.

"I can wear one of dem wedding dresses I got," she offered eagerly. "From the Thrift Shop."

"It was strange," Wendy said, "because although she had no use for men, she thought she would be married one day."

Wendy explained that wedding dresses were not a part of this show but said they would go shopping for the kind of clothing they would be exhibiting. Unfortunately when they found a suitable outfit at a consignment store in Gibsons, the clerks would not permit Bergie to try it on.

"We suggested a heavy fleece outfit," said Patti, "but Bergie found a twinkly skyscraper sweater that she liked better."

At the Saan store, Bergie insisted on steel-toe shoes, which she could use after the show. However, she did agree to the sports bra Wendy chose and was delighted by the black silk lace underwear they found.

Engine trouble made Bergie late in arriving at Patti Lunan's house on the morning of the fashion show.

"I had to jimmy up dat der boat," she said.

She was soon luxuriating in a bubble bath which, she declared, "would do Minnie's bones so good!"

Later, when Patti offered her hot scones instead of cake, she said, "I don't know why anyone would cook without sugar!" She was appeased by the addition of sugar and jam to the scone, and by having her clothes washed. Ever after, she saw Patti's house as a place where she could have her laundry done for free.

"I had to put a stop to that," Patti said.

Later, at the makeover event, although apparently pleased with the "gentle grandma" image created by the makeup crew, Bergie needed repeated reassurance that everything being done to her could be undone. At the last moment, she pulled out a bag of costume jewellery.

"Oh, sure," she said, slipping a sparkly bracelet onto her wrist. "Dese are pretty tings, too."

"You can't wear that jewellery, Bergie!" moaned Wendy. "There's no rhyme nor reason to it! And it doesn't go with the outfit!"

By this time the audience was growing restless and the town administrator, Joe Calenda, who was to be Bergie's escort, was waiting near the closed door, a bouquet of roses in his arms. Finally, in exasperation, Wendy threw up her arms.

The Cougar Lady, softened by a bubble bath and makeup for the Women in the Marketplace Fashion Show held at Sechelt's Rockwood Lodge, October 2006. Photo courtesy of Audrey Broughton.

Bergie refused to go onstage at the 2006 makeover event until she saw her sister, Minnie, seated in the audience. Photo courtesy of Audrey Broughton.

"All right!" she surrendered. "Keep the bracelet—but nothing else!"

Bergie smiled and, after a quick check to ensure that Minnie was seated in the audience, finally accepted the roses from Joe. Then, to the music of Natalie Cole's "Once in a Lifetime" and with the administrator at her side, she stepped into the spotlight.

The audience gasped. Before them was a pretty woman with stylishly curled honey-blond hair, standing poised and confident, a delighted smile softening her features. The dark cityscape pattern woven into her long, purple-hued sweater matched her fashionable black slacks, making her look almost tall and slender. She walked proudly to the stage, turned to face the audience and raised her hand in a salute reminiscent of the Queen Mother. Then with her escort she began a slow circuit of the room.

The spectators clapped and cheered, and, delighted by the applause, Bergie smiled broadly. Regally she presented a rose to a lady on her left, and then another to a lady on her right, repeating the action until her bouquet was exhausted. Finally Joe escorted her to a chair beside her sister.

Heavier than Bergie, Minnie was dressed all in black save for a mauve t-shirt that she wore over a long-sleeved top. Her head was covered by a round, black felt hat held in place by a cord fastened beneath her chin. As Bergie walked toward her, Minnie stared at her sister, her expression a mixture of envy and admiration.

"Minnie did compliment her," Wendy recalled, "but then *she* wanted a turn at looking pretty."

When it was apparent that this wasn't going to happen, Minnie became moody and began to complain.

"When the show was over, I made sure Bergie and Minnie had dinner," Wendy said. "Then I took them down to the wharf. As they got into the boat, they had this terrible argument. I can still hear them going up Porpoise Bay just a-screaming at each other in Norwegian."

For the most part, Bergie enjoyed her notoriety, and she was delighted when a photograph of her makeover appeared in the local paper. Her summary of the event was that it took a lot of work to be pretty, but she liked the feeling. A few days after the show Wendy asked her what she did with her clothes.

"Oh sure, I took dem home," Bergie responded. "I'm keeping dem for good." She wasn't even wearing her new steel-

Reassured that nothing had been done to her features that could not be undone, Bergie stood with town administrator Joe Calenda before a sellout crowd at Rockwood Lodge. Photo courtesy of Patti Lunan.

toe shoes because she didn't want them to get dirty.

Two months later Bergie came into Wendy's hairdressing shop. "She was really upset because somebody had stolen her silk underwear at the laundromat. She wanted me to drive her down to get some more." Wendy bought her six pairs of silk panties and replenished this supply every Christmas. "Nobody knew that under those rugged outfits Bergie wore expensive silk panties."

Wendy's eyes rolled as she described Bergie's single complaint about the fashion show. "For a whole year she would appear at the shop mad as all get-out because I had cut her bangs too short and she couldn't get her sparkly clip back in under her hat. So I had to buy her a new sparkly clip that would work."

Any lingering doubts Wendy had about the appropriateness of including Bergie in the show were dispelled that Christmas when she received a card in the mail. The message inside was spelled wrong, and some of the letters were backward. It read simply, "Thank You from Bergliot."

THE LAST OF A LEGEND

One day in the mid-1980s a car pulled up beside Bergie on Sechelt's main street. The driver, who introduced himself as Cliff Voth, asked if she was related to Minnie Solberg. When Bergie responded that she was Minnie's sister, the man introduced his wife, Lois, as Minnie's daughter and said that she had spent many years searching for her natural mother. Bergie told them where Minnie lived and the couple chartered a plane to Deserted Bay. They had been warned that if they weren't feeling like company, Minnie and Henry often disappeared into the backwoods when a plane or boat arrived. As a consequence, Lois was not sure if she would be greeted by her mother or be met with an empty house. To her relief, it was one of Minnie's sociable days.

"I was there when they met," said Wendell Welander. "You just looked at Lois and knew she was Minnie's daughter."

For many summers after that the Voths would bring their children to visit Minnie and Henry.

In 1989 Henry Dray succumbed to his heart condition, and Minnie was left alone in their Jervis Inlet home with almost no money until Jim Wilkinson helped her to obtain a widow's pension from the Department of Veterans Affairs. This gave her a guaranteed monthly income, which she augmented by trapping. Henry had willed his Deserted Bay trapline to her, and because it was closer to her home and she was not allowed to have two, she relinquished her own trapline between Salmon and Narrows inlets.

Still, Minnie never seemed to have quite enough to pay for the repairs on her boat, the fuel it took to travel back and forth from Sechelt, the feed for her goats, chickens and rabbits and her own groceries. Since Bergie was also living on a small pension and in the same position, the two often helped each other out, with either Bergie travelling up to Deserted Bay or Minnie travelling down to Carlson Creek. In Sechelt, Bergie was able to use her contacts to arrange rides for Minnie and the transport of her supplies to and from the wharf.

"One time I was going up Jervis Inlet and Bergie asked me to take Minnie a few things," wrote John Dafoe. "Every time I saw her she added to the load with an array of sweets and fatty foods that would be considered most unhealthy fare. Finally I got away and a good thing too or my little boat would not manage the load. We went up to a camp just past Deserted Bay and met Minnie on a [quad] that she drove to the beach. This mountain of a woman was quite a sight driving down to the landing on that machine. We explained our mission and were well-received by her and she wanted us to unload an oil barrel from a stand by her cabin. It appeared that the cabin was somewhat supported by the stand and barrel and we thought better of removing it. Minnie accepted our explanation."[48]

During these years Bergie continued to visit her friend, Dorothy Chamberlain Clode.

"She'd fly to Nanaimo on the Beaver airplane that was named after her," said Dorothy's daughter, Elizabeth. "We'd get a call that in an hour she was coming, and so we'd race to pick her up. But she could only stay a few hours because she had to get back to her goats. We'd stop at a store and get her new clothes because she wouldn't buy anything else. She'd have a bath and clean up, and we'd have a meal."

In the early 1980s, after Wilkinson established the radio in her cabin, Bergie became part of a CB group of about twelve people who talked to each other almost every day. Those who had nothing to say would still enjoy listening to the others. At times, when she was in the right mood, Bergie would entertain them with a song.

"She could sing and yodel a lot of Wilf Carter's old songs," said Wilkinson. "So we would get her to play her guitar and sing this song, with her Norwegian accent:

Oh it's cloudy in the vest
And it's lookin' like rain
The darned ol' slicker's in de vagon again
Come a ti yi yippi yippi yae yippi yae . . . ."

Once Bergie watched a television show in which someone was using a telephone that had a video monitor. When she told

Wilkinson about the show he remarked that he could see her on the CB.

"Oh, you're just joking," she said.

Encouraged by the doubt he detected in her voice, Wilkinson decided to push the joke a little farther. He called her early one winter morning and said, "It's so dark, I can hardly see you, Bergie!"

"Oh, gosh!" she exclaimed. "Should I light a lamp?"

"No, that's not really necessary," he returned.

By then Bergie had realized the joke.

"Oh, you can't see me!" she scoffed.

By this time Bergie was in her late sixties and her living conditions were beginning to deteriorate. Because her boat motors were old and constantly exposed to the salt air, they were always breaking down and needing repairs, which she could not afford. Too often she trusted the wrong people to do her repairs, resulting in a dispute over the amount they charged. When she did go to a reliable dealer, she was so accustomed to being cheated that she often refused to pay the full amount for labour and parts. The dealers would hold her repaired motor hostage, and though her relentless pestering eventually caused them to give it back, they refused to do any further work on her behalf.

One mechanic who lived on a houseboat at the Porpoise Bay wharf often helped Bergie and Minnie out.

"He was very good at fixing old motors," said Jim Wilkinson. "Their motors were old and worn out, but he'd fix them up for free, and then they would complain that he hadn't done a good job. So he stopped fixing them."

At Carlson Creek Bergie's cabin roof leaked and the propane cook stove she was using for heat created a perpetual dampness. Her goat sheds were falling apart and the wharf she used to get to and from her boat was rotting and missing boards. Finally, she decided that moving across the creek to Piper Point and building a new cabin would solve all of her problems.

Entrance to Bergie's cabin. Bergie's cabin at Carlson Creek overflowed with paraphernalia that she saved in case there were ever again shortages such as those experienced during World War II. Photo courtesy of Oddvin Vedo, oddvinvedo.wordpress.com.

Since Piper Point was not part of Dorothy Chamberlain Clode's property, Bergie needed permission from the provincial government to settle there. To obtain this, she decided to transfer her trapline to the west side of the inlet. Fortunately, there was a trapline that was no longer being used that included Piper Point, and on July 23, 1990, with considerable help from conservation officer Doug Pierce and the staff at the Ministry of Environment, she officially made the change. It was only after the trapline had been transferred that Bergie discovered there were stipulations to erecting a trapper's cabin and they did not include full-time occupation. Then Minnie became ill, and all of Bergie's energies were suddenly focussed on her sister.

One June day in 1995 Minnie arrived in Sechelt to visit Bergie and to replenish her supplies at Deserted Bay. It was the first trip to town that she'd made in three months and by the time she headed back home the boat was fully loaded. That evening, when Minnie failed to radio that she had arrived safely, Bergie got worried and alerted the police. "Wednesday morning," wrote Nancy Moote in *Coastlife*, "a helicopter search and rescue team found Minnie at Brittain River up the Prince of Wales Reach, approximately 50 km from Sechelt and halfway from Egmont to her home at Deserted Bay. She had put in there for the night, apparently because of engine trouble. Bergie … said she's never been worried like this in the thirty years that her sister has lived at Deserted Bay."[49]

In a later interview, Moote asked Bergie why she and Minnie didn't move in together.

> "I asked Minnie she should move down to my place," [Bergie] laughs, "[but] she said why don't you move up to my place?'
>
> So the two independent sisters continue to live their separate lives. They talk by radio phone and visit occasionally.
>
> "People told us to live in Sechelt, in an old people's home," says Solberg. "That's the last place I'll go. I don't want to sit and look at the walls. I want to be out in the bush and go hunting and trapping. To be free."[50]

Although she had struggled valiantly to remain in Jervis Inlet, Minnie had developed a heart condition, diabetes and, eventually, ulcerations on her legs for which she was hospitalized many times. Like her parents, she hated the hospital and fought to get out from the minute she was admitted. Often, to keep her angry shouting from disturbing the rest of the patients, she was moved to a distant part of the ward. Time after time, just as the ulcers in her legs would begin to heal, she would insist on going home and Bergie would talk someone into driving to the hospital to pick her up and take her down to the boat. This was a difficult task because Minnie had grown very heavy, and between her ulcerated leg and her weight she often needed help in and out of vehicles. Still, she would hobble down to her boat and head back to Jervis Inlet, and when it became impossible for her to look after herself there, she went to Carlson Creek.

Now in her seventies, Bergie could still haul green bales of hay or alfalfa down to the wharf. She would stand the bale up on the tailgate of whatever vehicle had delivered it, then turn around and slip her hands under the upper cord holding the bale together and let it fall onto her back. Stooped forward, she would carry it down the ramp to her boat. At Carlson Creek she would carry the bale from her boat, along her rickety wharf and up to the goat sheds. After her wharf was reduced to a single log from the dock to the shore, she broke the bales apart and hauled them up in smaller bunches.

But hay bales were not the only things that Bergie hauled down to the wharf.

"Minnie and Bergie had two eighty-pound propane bottles," said Wendell Welander. "They came in one day with the two bottles for refill and Bergie was struggling to get them out of her boat. I'd been having problems with my back so I grabbed one of the guys to help me. The bottles were long and awkward to carry, but we each grabbed an end of one, carried it up the

Bergie loved her independence, but living alone amid the rustic conditions at Carlson Creek was not easy. Eventually age and arthritis took their toll on her health, and by then she was using a propane stove for heat and trying to cope with a leaky roof, disintegrating animal shelters and a rotting dock. Photo courtesy of Bill Walkey.

ramp and threw it in the pickup. Then we looked behind us and here comes Bergie with the other bottle!"

Age and arthritis, however, were also taking a toll on Bergie's health. Her hands swelled to twice their normal size and caused her constant pain, especially in winter. Not that she let this stop her from running her boat back and forth to Sechelt.

"If she didn't have a boat motor that ran, she rowed," said Jim Wilkinson. "I remember looking out my window one afternoon about three o'clock and she was coming down the inlet, bucking a wind. She would row and row and row, and then she would stop and rest and the wind would blow her back, and then she would row again. Well, after this went on for an hour, I couldn't stand it any longer. So I went down to my boat, motored over and threw her a rope and pulled her into Sechelt. You couldn't defeat her. She wasn't afraid to do anything."

As Bergie and Minnie's needs increased and the physical pain they were both experiencing caused their tempers to shorten, the Solberg sisters began to antagonize the local merchants.

"Sometimes Bergie would get a little bossy," said Shirley Lewis. "One day I went to the bank for Tyee and as I was returning to work she flagged me down and asked for a ride."

Assuming that the ride requested was back to her boat, Lewis started driving in that direction.

"No! No!" Bergie cried. "You've got to turn here to go to Gibsons."

"I can't," said Lewis. "I've got to go to work."

But Bergie was insistent. "You've gotta take me to Quality Farms in Gibsons!"

"My boss will have my job if I do that," Lewis told her, and continued on down to the wharf. "Bergie was mad at me for a while after that."

Although Bergie was very protective of her own things and threatened to shoot anyone who came near her property, she assumed that she was free to use the facilities of any public enterprise. When the late William "Bert" Shaw became caretaker of the Clowhom Dam, now owned by BC Hydro, his job included the maintenance of the hydro boat and he spent hours of his own time making sure that both the vessel and its engine were as clean as the day they left the factory. One afternoon he returned to the Sechelt wharf to find Bergie on board, along with four bales of hay and two goats.

"What the hell is this?" he demanded.

She responded that she wanted him to take the goats to Poise Island where they could graze, and then take her and the hay to Carlson Creek.

"No bloody way!" Shaw exploded. "I'm not running a taxi service."

"Oh, gosh," Bergie said, shaking her head sorrowfully. "I don't know what I can do den." Then she looked at him sharply. "The other guy always took my goats."

"Well, I'm not the other guy," Shaw snorted. "So get this stuff off my boat."

"Gosh," Bergie said again, "I guess I can't do that."

"You do that or I'm throwing the hay *and* the goats into the chuck," Shaw snapped.

After several more minutes of wrangling during which Bergie showed no inclination to remove herself, her goats or her hay, Shaw lost patience. Picking up the nearest bale, he tossed it overboard. Bergie yelled and scrambled to the dock where she was able to retrieve the bale.

"Get them off my boat, or I'm tossing the rest in with it!" Shaw ordered.

Glowering and muttering about "miserable peoples," Bergie hoisted the hay bales and goats onto the dock.

"For a whole bloody year after that," grumbled Shaw, "I was cleaning hay out of the bilge!"

The airline office was another public service that the Solbergs believed was theirs to enjoy.

"In the winter," said Shirley Lewis, "Bergie would moor her boat, then come into our waiting room and sit and drink our coffee until she got warm. If there was no coffee made, she'd knock on the door and say, 'There's no coffee. You better make some.' We had a donation cup for the coffee, but she never paid."

When Wendell Welander took over controlling interest of Coast Western Airlines he often saw Minnie and Bergie in the office, filling their pockets with sugar lumps. He knew that Minnie suffered from diabetes and that raw sugar was the worst thing she could eat. To put a stop to the habit he substituted the cubes with granulated sugar in a jar, but to no avail.

"They just put handfuls of sugar in their pockets," he said.

One day a friend borrowed Welander's truck and in exchange Welander drove the friend's car, a fancy 1998 Oldsmobile.

"I gave Minnie and Bergie a ride to town and there was sugar leaking from their pockets, along with dog hair and goat hair from their clothes. It took me an hour to clean that car!"

Because they'd never owned a functioning automobile of their own, neither sister could understand why some people were so passionate about the care of their vehicles. Nor could they understand when their friends began to resent the time and gas money it took to transport them and their supplies to and from the stores.

Among the numerous local residents who gave Bergie rides, John Alvarez earned a permanent spot in the well-worn pages of her address book.

"Whenever you were dealing with Bergie," he said, "you had to be cautious. She was so determined to accomplish whatever it was she had set out to do that you could find yourself in serious trouble if you didn't take the time to learn all the facts about what she wanted before you started out."

Bergie often navigated Sechelt Inlet by rowboat, even in her old age. Author photo.

One spring day Bergie had an opportunity to sell her extra billy goat to a buyer in Madeira Park, but the billy was too big and too mean for her to risk transporting it in her boat. Instead she called Alvarez and asked if he could bring his four-wheel-drive pickup down the back road to Carlson Creek and collect the goat for her. Reluctantly, he agreed. He met Bergie in Sechelt and together they drove to Halfmoon Bay and onto the logging road, which was just barely passable. As they neared Carlson Creek, they were suddenly faced with a steep mudbank that led down to a marshy patch of ground. They were still more than fifteen metres away from the fenced area containing the billy goat, but Alvarez brought the truck to a halt. He got out and inspected the ground, then shook his head.

"I can't drive through that, Bergie."

"Oh sure," Bergie protested. "I got some plywood. We can lay it down on top." She trudged through the muck, returning with two sheets of quarter-inch plywood.

Again Alvarez shook his head.

"Truck'll go right through that."

Bergie wasn't happy, but she knew he wasn't about to change his mind. She had planned to put a nanny into the truck box and use it to lure the billy inside. That trick, however, would not work over such a long distance. Reluctantly, she got into the truck and they drove back to Sechelt.

The next day she rowed across the inlet to the Tillicum Bay marina and called Alvarez again.

"Oh gosh," she said, "I've got a terrible time here."

It turned out that she had persuaded the owner of a small van to drive to Carlson Creek with her to pick up the goat. On the way the van's transmission had been damaged, and when they reached the marshy ground, the vehicle became stuck in the mud.

"Sure, maybe you could come and give us a tow out of there," she begged Alvarez.

Knowing his old truck was not up to such a task, he told her she needed a big tow truck. When she claimed she had no more quarters, he called the towing company for her, then drove to Tillicum Bay, collected Bergie and took her to Sechelt, where she met the tow-truck driver.

A week later Alvarez spoke to Bergie in Sechelt and learned that all the time she had been arranging for the tow truck, the billy and nanny goat had been in the van that was stuck in the mud back at Carlson Creek.

"That rig wasn't as good as yours," she said. "The tow truck had to tow us all the way to Madeira Park. Gosh, that cost a lot."

Bigpacific.com webmaster Laurie McConnell describes how Bergie would obtain rides to and from the dock.

> A common trick of Bergie's that many fell for, myself included, was to sidle up to a car getting filled up at the Shell station in the centre of town, and say in her Norwegian-accented mumble, "... get a ride to them docks in Porpoise Bay?" An initial recoil from the surprise of the request from a complete stranger would evolve into the mental gymnastics of figuring that everyone knew her ... though she was seen as wild and a bit barmy by some there was an implied sense of safety in saying yes, after all, didn't I see her in John's truck just last week?
>
> So, the Samaritan says yes, and Bergie says, "Be right back. Gettin' ma bags," and then would proceed to disappear and do all her grocery shopping now that a ride was assured! You'd wait in your car, feeling absurdly obligated to hold to your word even though she'd clearly changed the terms from her side, watching 15 minutes, and then 30 and finally perhaps 45 minutes go by. Eventually she'd amble and hitch her way across the crosswalks from Clayton's with her foodstuffs—or ask you to drive over to the store entrance to pick everything up—and you'd pack the food, Bergie and a few full cans of gas into your car and

> off you'd go to the docks, an olfactory extravaganza wafting through town.[51]

While many local citizens felt sorry for Bergie and Minnie and went out of their way to help them, not everyone was sympathetic toward their plight. Some local merchants denied them access to their stores simply because it was too expensive to allow them to enter. It wasn't unheard of for the sisters to open containers and sample their contents or to come to town with their clothes reeking of the skunk they'd just cleaned and stop to eat at a restaurant.

"Bergie and Minnie used to eat at my shop," said Faye Hansen, who once owned a bulk food store and lunch counter in Sechelt. "But a lot of people wouldn't come in when they were there."

In the summer 2003 edition of the *Sunshine Coast Visitor's Guide*, Leonor Luzardo wrote that Ye Old English Doughnut Shoppe, owned by Bergie's friend Maria Garcia, was one of Bergie's customary stops every time she came to town.

> She always liked her coffee served in a "purdy" cup and if someone new at the doughnut shop served it in a regular cup—they heard about it.

Luzardo also wrote that Maria called Bergie the "Let's make a deal lady," and said,

> She'd come in every day and look at the day-old doughnuts and ask, "Are these free?" I'd tell her how much they were and she'd say, "That much!"[52]

Patti Lunan believes that for Bergie and Minnie, bargaining and getting the better of a deal was their way of surviving. "If Bergie could get a free cup of coffee by claiming it was cold, that was just a way to get an extra sixty cents in her pocket."

Among the merchants the sisters quarrelled with were the volunteer staff of the St. Mary's Hospital Auxiliary Thrift Store. Already angry and distrustful of the hospital, Bergie and Minnie believed that because the merchandise in the thrift shop had been donated, the Hospital Auxiliary had no right to charge for it.

"They drove the volunteers crazy," said Betty Laidlaw. "They would pick everything over, then bring it to the counter and try to bargain for a lower price. Sometimes they would be quite abusive and intimidate the women there."

Jo Hammond was once delivering a supply of used clothing to the thrift store when she was waylaid by Minnie and Bergie, who wanted to inspect everything Jo was donating.

"I had about four bags of clothes," said Jo, "and they insisted that I take everything out and lay it on the ground. They were quite rude with their remarks, saying things like, 'I wouldn't put that on my cat!' Then they went away and I had to pick everything up and put it back again."

One day while she went off to purchase gas and groceries, Bergie left Minnie sitting in a secluded corner in the thrift shop. Minnie fell asleep and the volunteers, assuming Bergie had retrieved her, closed the shop and went home. When Bergie returned to collect her sister, the door was locked and it took several frantic phone calls before someone arrived to open the door. Bergie never forgave the volunteers for imprisoning her sister and thereafter shared her hatred of the thrift shop with anyone who would listen.

There were times, however, when Bergie carried her vendettas too far.

"When Bergie got mad, she'd threaten you," said Shirley Lewis. "Once when I told her she couldn't use the phone anymore, she got mad and said she'd hang me in the airplane hangar!"

After another altercation, she had to post a $250 peace bond for six months.

An even more serious charge might have occurred after an altercation on the Sechelt wharf in the 1990s had a friend not stepped in to help.

At that time Bergie was having trouble keeping Herman's old boat, the *Fjeld*, afloat. She had never used it much herself, preferring a smaller craft with an outboard engine, but because her father had built it, she kept the *Fjeld* anchored in Chamberlain Bay. Now it was leaking too much for her to continue anchoring it, and in desperation she contacted William Griffith in Egmont.

"Gosh, if you don't buy the boat," she said, "I'll have to give it to you. It costs too much for me to pay wharfage."

For years Griffith had been collecting motors and other antique items for what would eventually become the Egmont Heritage Centre.[53] He already owned an old hand-cranked jack and a couple of air-cooled engines that had once belonged to Herman, as well as the *Fjeld's* original Vivian engine. Since the vessel's Easthope engine was still in running condition, he offered to pay Bergie four hundred dollars for the boat—two hundred more than she was asking.

"I know she would have given it to me if I didn't buy it," he said, "but I don't deal with people that way."

Griffith arranged to collect the *Fjeld* from the loading dock in Sechelt. Eager to complete the deal, Bergie towed it over long before he was due to arrive, and while she was waiting there, a landing barge pulled up to the dock but couldn't land. Furious with Bergie for taking up all the room, the barge pilot docked at the public wharf, then stomped over, untied the *Fjeld* and pushed it away from the loading dock. As Bergie scrambled to retie the boat, the barge owner began yelling at her. John Alvarez arrived about that time and was watching the battle with some amusement. Suddenly the barge owner swung around and began screaming at Alvarez for grinning.

"The biggest problem I had," said Alvarez, "was trying to talk fast enough to calm Bergie down because by then she was standing behind him with a club. I really didn't want her to hit him."

Bergie's frustrations increased as her sister's health continued to fail. Although Minnie once had a good command of the English language, her hearing had deteriorated to the point where she could no longer understand what people were saying. As a consequence, she began using only Norwegian, and it was left to Bergie to make arrangements for her care, a task that became increasingly difficult.

"Minnie was so nasty with Bergie," said Wendell Welander, "likely because she was in pain all the time. Most people didn't realize that about her. Minnie used to be a lot different. But Bergie would come in every day when Minnie was in hospital. Even when the weather wasn't safe for travelling she'd come in with fresh goat's milk and creek water, because that was all Minnie would drink."

Bill Walkey arrived early at Carlson Creek to photograph Bergie and caught her combing her hair. It was one of the few times he'd ever seen her smile. Photo courtesy of Bill Walkey.

"She even convinced Maria [Garcia] to cook oysters for Minnie (her favourite food cooked in butter), which she did often. Minnie didn't like hospital food," wrote Leonor Luzardo.[54]

One of the hardest problems Bergie faced was finding a place for Minnie to stay when she was not in the hospital. The dock at Carlson Creek rested on mudflats at low tide and at times the sisters would have to wait out in the bay until after midnight for the tide to come in and float the dock enough for Minnie to walk to shore. The cabin roof leaked and when it rained the beds would be soaking wet and cold.

"Sometimes I shleep in the chair all night," said Bergie.

To make things easier for Minnie, Bergie contacted Betty Laidlaw, who was in charge of St. Mary's Hospital Loan Cupboard.

"She inquired about getting a hospital bed for Minnie," said Betty, "but I knew she would have to take it over to her place by boat."

When Laidlaw asked why she needed the bed, Bergie responded, "Oh, gosh, this place has no beds. It's okay for me to sleep on the floor, but Minnie can't get up and down because of her leg."

"Fortunately," said Laidlaw, "all of our beds were out just then."

Several times Bergie induced her friends to take her sister in, but Minnie's increasing lack of hygiene, which included spitting on the floor and refusing to take a bath, discouraged them from having her stay for more than a few days at a time. For a while Minnie went to stay with her daughter in Armstrong and when that didn't work out she was installed in a nearby nursing home.

For the old trapper this was an unbearable prison, and as soon as she was able to escape, Minnie walked away from the home, got on a bus and returned to Sechelt.

Bergie had missed Minnie while she was with Lois and was constantly calling her. The owners of a small grocery store in Sechelt often let Bergie use their phone. One day Betty Laidlaw happened to mention to them that Minnie was in Armstrong and that Bergie was complaining because she had to send nine hundred dollars each month to the nursing home, which only left her seven hundred dollars for her own expenses.

"Armstrong?" gasped the store owner. "Is that where the calls are going to on my telephone bill?"

When Betty saw him a few days later she jokingly asked if Bergie was still calling Armstrong on his bill.

"No," he said. "Now when she wants the phone we give her twenty-five cents and tell her to use the pay phone."

Minnie stayed with Bergie for a while after her return from Armstrong, but once again she refused to keep the bandages on her legs or clean the ulcerated areas, and soon they became badly infected. By the time Minnie was in enough pain and discomfort that she was willing to return to the hospital, she was almost delirious and no longer able to walk. She was far too heavy to be carried, so Bergie called emergency services, which resulted in a helicopter crew coming to pick her up. At the hospital they warned Bergie that such an expensive rescue would not be forthcoming the next time she called.

Once again Jim Wilkinson came to the Solbergs' aid and, with support from others in the community, arranged for Minnie to obtain a room at the Green Court assisted living complex.

"We went to the Salvation Army and bought some used furniture," said Wilkinson, "and because she was the widow of a veteran, the Legion came up with an emergency fund of five hundred dollars to buy the necessary pots and pans she needed."

Minnie was released from hospital, but she was furious when Bergie refused to take her up the inlet and immediately began finding fault with her room at Green Court.

"So we got her into Shorncliffe," said Wilkinson. "But she was in there for just one night and she just got up and walked out. We got her back into Green Court and I think she lived there about a week, but she didn't like it."

Wilkinson was checking on Minnie each day to see if she needed anything. When he arrived one morning and Minnie wasn't there, he immediately went to his CB and called Bergie.

"Oh sure," Bergie said. "She came home with me last night."

As expected, it was not long before Minnie's ulcers became infected, and once again, with the help of police and ambulance personnel who agreed to go over in a boat to get her, she was returned to the hospital. Unfortunately, this time it was too late. On September 2, 2001, at the age of seventy-nine, Minnie died at St. Mary's Hospital in Sechelt.

With Minnie's death a great deal of life seemed to disappear from Bergie. She still spoke of moving to Piper Point, but there was not the same conviction in her voice. Her movements were slower, and she laughed less. As she had with her parents, she blamed the hospital, the doctors and the nurses for her sister's death, but she also blamed herself. She worried that if she'd only had her place fixed up better, Minnie might have been able to stay there more comfortably.

The following spring Mike Jackson and Jim Wilkinson drove to Carlson Creek, braving the rugged back road, to visit Bergie.

"Things were in pretty sad shape," said Jackson. "The cabin door wouldn't shut, and the wind was blowing through. But after her sister died Bergie just went downhill."

Bergie's sadness increased in February 2002 when she learned that her old friend Dorothy Clode had died. Mixed with her sadness was concern that she might be evicted from the Carlson Creek property. Fortunately, when she contacted the family they reassured her that she could stay, and a few weeks later their property manager, Jerry Joyce, came to Sechelt to help her out.

"Bergie was in dire straits," he said. "Her toilet was a small canvass shelter around a bucket that had a seat on it."

After his visit, the Clode family purchased a new outboard motor for her, had a new roof put on her shack and installed a new float.

"They dropped anchors from it," said Joyce. "Way more than it needed, but Bergie insisted on it."

Unfortunately, the improvements to her living conditions did nothing to raise her spirits, which seemed to grow even dimmer in the gathering darkness of the oncoming winter. And one cold day, even Jim Wilkinson was unable to rouse her.

Ever since he'd installed a CB in Bergie's cabin, Wilkinson had made a point of calling frequently to make sure she was okay; after Minnie died, he called every day. He saw Bergie on the morning of November 11, 2002, but when he called her that evening, there was no answer. He tried again the following morning and still received no response. Deciding something must be wrong with her CB, he asked his son-in-law,

Although Bergie (right) and others found Minnie (left) several places to live in town, she would invariably turn up at Carlson Creek and beg to be taken to Deserted Bay. She died on September 2, 2001, and a great deal of life seemed to disappear from Bergie. Photo December 2000, courtesy of Jan DeGrass.

Steve Day, to take his boat to Carlson Creek to see if everything was all right.

"I went close to the shore," said Day. "It was low tide and the dog was barking, which wasn't unusual. But the boat was up on the beach and it didn't look right, so I went up to the house."

He found Bergie inside, on the floor. She had been cooking supper when she collapsed and died.

Day returned to Sechelt to pick up two RCMP officers and take them to Carlson Creek.

"They were dressed in their fancy uniforms and shoes and had no gumboots," he said. "I told them they needed gumboots to get to Bergie's cabin at low tide. But they waded across the muck in their shoes."

An hour later Day helped the officers carry Bergie's body to his boat and transport it to Sechelt.

"It was Bergie's last ride on the inlet," he said quietly.

More than one hundred people came out to the Seaview Cemetery in Gibsons and stood in the cold November rain as Bergie's coffin was lowered into the ground beside her sister. Nearby were the graves of Herman and Olga.

The occasion marked the end of the remarkable life of a character not moulded by schools or church or books or television, but by the ruggedness of the land and the weather and the animals she hunted and cared for. Those who knew her well, who liked and admired her, saw beyond her rough edges, beyond her temper and her unconventional behaviour. They saw the courage and endurance she displayed every time she ventured out onto a cold, unpredictable inlet and without

Those who knew Bergie well saw beyond her rough edges. Photo courtesy of Bill Walkey.

hesitation headed for a distant landing such as the end of Narrows Inlet, where she'd walk for miles up rugged mountain slopes searching for a goat or a deer or a cougar. With equal ease, she would guide her boat through the Skookumchuck Rapids and up Jervis Inlet to Deserted Bay to visit her sister.

Bergliot Solberg was a woman who acknowledged no boundaries, who was, in her own way, as wild as the eagle that soars above the sea or the silent cougar that prowls the forest.

She had touched the lives of many and she left an emptiness with her dying.

The mourners returned to their cars and drove to the Sechelt Legion, where one by one they stood in front of the crowd and with tears, laughter and caring, told their own stories of the Cougar Lady of Sechelt Inlet.

ACKNOWLEDGEMENTS

Bergliot Solberg could not have lived the kind of life she did without the support of her community. This same community helped me compile her history by providing leads, anecdotes, stories and pictures. Though many members of this community, like Bergie and Minnie, are no longer living, I am grateful for their input.

I am especially grateful to John Alvarez, Bill Bestwick, David Birdsall, John Bosch, Don Brinton, Audrey Broughton, William "Grizz" Burt, Eirwen Cleaver, Elizabeth Clode, Ken Collins, Cavin Crawford, Doris Crowston, Rudy Crucil, John Dafoe, Faith (Elvin) Darnbrought, Steve Day, Dr. T. Gerry Egan, Richard Elvin, Frieda Fawkes, William "Billy" Griffith, Jo and Richard "Dick" Hammond, Faye (Wood) Hansen, Margaret "Peggy" Hemstreet, Mike Jackson, Pete Jackson, Norm Johnson, Jerry Joyce, Ed and Betty Laidlaw, Holly Pratt Lehman, Robert "Bob" and Kaye Lemieux, Roberta (Pratt) Leslie, Shirley Lewis, Rod Lizee, Patti Lunan, Roland Lussier, Laurie McConnell,

Ian Munro, Joan O'Shea, Dr. Eric Paetkau, George Page, Sheila Page, Thomas "Tom" Parish, Donald Ream Jr., Dean Robilliard, Dorothy Robilliard, William "Bert" Shaw, Tor Skei, Diane Sperring, James A. Stephen Jr., Ray Stockwell, Dr. Alan Swan, Keith Thirkell, Rose Tonders, Oddvin Vedo, Bill Walkey, Wendell Welander, Jim Wilkinson, Alan Wood, Wendy Young.

I am also indebted to Ann Watson, Janet Ansell and Val Swanson of the Sechelt Community Archives; Kimiko Hawkes and Mathew Lovegrove of the Sunshine Coast Museum and Archives; Jack Evans, senior wildlife biologist, Fish and Wildlife Branch, Government of British Columbia; Angela Montgomery, Citizenship and Immigration Canada; and Peter F. Olesiuk, marine mammal biologist, Department of Fisheries and Oceans.

ENDNOTES

1 T.K. Derry, *A History of Modern Norway 1814–1977*. Oxford: Clarendon Press, 1973.

2 Janet E. Rasmussen, *New Land, New Lives: Scandinavian Immigrants to the Pacific Northwest*. Seattle: University of Washington Press, 1993.

3 The Emergency Quota Act of 1921 limited the number of immigrants from a given country entering the United States in any one year to 3 percent of the number of immigrants from that country that had been living in the United States in 1910.

4 F.C. Mears, "Steamship Combine Is Stifling Canada in Trade Expansion. Report of W.T.R. Preston, Tabled in House of Commons," *Globe and Mail*, February 10, 1925, p. 1.

5 Ninette Kelley and Michael Trebilcock, *The Making of the Mosaic: A History of Canadian Immigration Policy.* Toronto: University of Toronto Press, 1998.

6 "Simple Conditions Canada Demands From Settlers," *Globe and Mail*, June 11, 1925, p. 12.

7 Kelley and Trebilcock, *Mosaic.*

8 Nancy Moote, "Sechelt's Cougar Lady Likes Her Independence," *Coastlife*, June 19, 1995.

9 Ethel C. Burnett, "Fifteen Thousand MIlk Goats Raised in British Columbia," *Globe and Mail*, December 30, 1925, p. 8.

10 Moote, "Sechelt's Cougar Lady Likes Her Independence."

11 South MacKenzie Electoral District, BC, "Public Works Report," *Sessional Papers*, 1936–7.

12 Rhody Lake, "Woman of the Woods," *Vancouver Sun*, July 5, 1975, p. 37.

13 Province of British Columbia, "Application of a Trap-Line," RM106, October 31, 1935.

14 A shook mill cuts and prepares boards for boxes.

15 R.B. Harvey, "Howe Sound Copper and Silver Mine," *Report of the Ministry of Mines*, Victoria, BC, June 26, 1877.

16 Eric Paetkau, interview with author, September 25, 2003. Story included in Eric J. Paetkau, *The Doc's Side: Tales of a Sunshine Coast Doctor*. Madeira Park, BC: Harbour Publishing, 2011.

17 Rick Antonson, Mary Trainer and Brian Antonson, *Slumach's Gold: In Search of a Legend*. Surrey, BC: Heritage House, 2007.

18 Clyde Gilmour, "Hoodoo Gold." *Vancouver Daily Province*, January 18, 1947, magazine section, p. 1.

19 Lake, "Woman of the Woods."

20 Ibid.

21 Bergliot Solberg, interview with author, May 4, 1991.

22 Donald Ream Jr., "The Cougar Sisters: A Brief Review from Portals of the Past," *BC Forest History Newsletter* No.75, Forest History Association of BC, December 2004.

23 Lake, "Woman of the Woods."

24 Peter F. Olesiuk, marine mammal biologist, Department of Fisheries and Oceans, email to the author.

25 "Last Ride," *Peninsula Times,* April 29, 1964, p. 9.

26 Moote, "Sechelt's Cougar Lady Likes Her Independence."

27 "Cougar Attacks Woman Hunter Five Miles from Town in Early Sunday Morning Dawn," *Peninsula Times,* May 29, 1968, p. 1.

28 "Seasoned Hunter," *Peninsula Times,* April 12, 1972, p. 1.

29 "Cougar Lady," CBC Television News Centre, December 24, 1986.

30 Moote, "Sechelt's Cougar Lady Likes Her Independence."

31 "Sechelt Provincial Court," *Peninsula Times,* October 31, 1979, p. B6.

32 J.A. Stephen Jr., conservation officer, Sechelt detachment, "Report of Crown Counsel," 1982.

33 Ibid.

34 Ibid.

35 Alice French, *Coast News,* April 17, 1952.

36 Dick Proctor, "Sunshine Coastings," the *Peninsula Times,* November 7, 1973, p. A6.

37 "Letters to the Editor," *Peninsula Times*, January 9, 1974.

38 Lake, "Woman of the Woods."

39 "Assault Charge," *Peninsula Times*, November 9, 1966, p. 1.

40 Jerry McIntosh, "The Best Years," CBC (1986).

41 Oddvin Vedo, "'Cougar-Lady'—Bergie—'I have eaten Cougars… they taste okay,'" Oddvin Vedo, http://oddvinvedo.wordpress.com/2012/02/09/cougar-lady-borgie-and-minnie-sechelt-inlet/ (accessed March 21, 2012).

42 *On The Road Again*, Show #7, 1988/89 series, hosted by Wayne Rostad, CBC ©1987. Song lyrics written by Wayne Rostad, Stag Creek Publishing, SOCAN.

43 Moote, "Sechelt's Cougar Lady Likes Her Independence."

44 Carl Christmas, "Voices up the Inlet," *Coast News Weekender*, October 1, 1992.

45 Brian Lee, "Mountain Minnie and the Cougar Lady" (editorial), *Harbour Spiel Online*, January 1, 2011.

46 Anna Diehl, "Gotta Get Their Goats," the *Reporter*, March 30, 1998.

47 Jan DeGrass, "'Cougar Ladies' on the Prowl for New Sechelt Home," *Coast Independent*, December 31, 2000, p. 15.

48 Ream, "The Cougar Sisters: A Brief Review from the Portals of the Past."

49 Nancy Moote, "Cougar Lady's Sister Safe and Sound," *Coastlife*, June 12, 1995, p. 6.

50 Moote, "Sechelt's Cougar Lady Likes Her Independence."

51 Laurie McConnell, "Remembering 'the Cougar Lady,'" Bigpacific.com, http://www.bigpacific.com/sunshinecoastmagazine/2011/02/28/remembering-the-cougar-lady/

52 Leonor Luzardo, "An Era on the Sunshine Coast Ends," *Sunshine Coast Visitor's Guide*, summer 2003, p. 13.

53 Opened in 2005, the Egmont Heritage Centre is located across the road from the Skookumchuck Narrows Provincial Park entrance.

54 Leonor Luzardo, "An Era on the Sunshine Coast Ends."

INDEX

ABOUT THE AUTHOR

Rosella Leslie has been writing since she was old enough to put thoughts on paper. She has published three novels: *The Goat Lady's Daughter* (2006), *Drift Child* (2010) and *The Federov Legacy* (2013). Her non-fiction work includes *The Sunshine Coast: A Place to Be* (2001), and she co-authored *Bright Seas, Pioneer Spirits: A History of the Sunshine Coast* (1996, 2009), *Sea-Silver: Inside British Columbia's Salmon-Farming Industry* (1996) and a BC Book Prize winner, *A Stain Upon the Sea: West Coast Salmon Farming* (2004). Her work has appeared in numerous magazines and newspapers, including *Western People* magazine and the *Leader*.